Charny's Men-at-Arms

Questions Concerning the Joust, Tournaments, and War

Steven Muhlberger

Wheaton, Illinois

Freelance Academy Press, Inc., Wheaton, IL 60189
www.freelanceacademypress.com

Printed in the United States of America
by Publishers' Graphics

21 20 19 18 17 16 15 14 13 12   1 2 3 4 5

ISBN 978-1-937439-05-7

Library of Congress Control Number: 2014932140

CONTENTS

ACKNOWLEDGEMENTS

I have been thinking about Geoffroi de Charny and his *Questions* for years, and in that time I have incurred a number of scholarly debts, which I am glad to acknowledge here.

First, my great gratitude to the many friends, acquaintances, and strangers who at one time or another have tried to interpret or translate or even answer any of the *Questions*. Thanks for sharing your enthusiasm.

Early on I was encouraged by Kelly DeVries and Richard Kaeuper to have faith in the value of this research.

Several people have been willing to look closely at some of the most difficult of the *Questions*, and their efforts were very helpful. These include Christos Nüssli, Xavier Nègre, and Alain Rey and two colleagues at Nipissing University, Derek Neal and Kelly Morris. Daniel E. O'Sullivan, S.N. Rosenberg and Christos Nüssli wrestled in particular with the case of the beautiful destrier, the grammatical structure of which, alas, still lacks its Sherlock Holmes.

Will McLean has offered a number of worthwhile insights and suggestions. Both Will and Ian Hargrove read and commented on the manuscript at an early stage.

I have benefited from institutional support as well. Nipissing University and its Faculty of Arts and Science granted me a much-appreciated sabbatical in 2009–10. Certain French Internet resources, primarily Gallica at the *Bibliothèque National de France* and various dictionaries at ATILF made my life much easier and the project practical. Thanks, France!

Finally I am grateful to my family for their support, interest and encouragement. I like to think that my parents in particular would have appreciated this book as much as they did the earlier ones.

ABBREVIATIONS

I have used the following designations to distinguish the entire Charny text on the law of arms, its three sections, and the constituent questions, whose numbering follows the edition of Michael Anthony Taylor:

Questions: The *Questions Concerning the Joust, Tournaments, and War*
Questions on the Joust: the first twenty questions, identified here as J1...J20
Questions on Tournaments: the next twenty-one questions, T1...T21
Questions on War: the final ninety-three questions, W1...W93

In the translation of the War section I have included a question found in the Madrid manuscript and incorporated in notes to the Rossbach edition, though not in the Taylor edition. I have identified it as W80A. The margin of the Madrid MS also provides us with an answer to question W44, also included in my translation.

Froissart: Jean Froissart, *Oeuvres,* ed. Kervyn de Lettenhove. 25 vols. (Brussels: Académie Royale des Sciences, des Lettres et des Beaux-Arts de Belgique, 1867–77).

Johnes: Jean Froissart, *Chronicles,* trans. Thomas Johnes. 2 vols. (London: H.G. Bohn, 1862).

1 INTRODUCTION

The *Questions Concerning the Joust, Tournaments, and War* is a lost classic work of European chivalry. It is the only record we have of a dramatic occasion when crucial questions on the nature of war and the proper conduct of the warrior's life—one definition of chivalry—were posed to an audience of experts, professional men-at-arms of rank and influence. Unfortunately the record is far from complete, and we must imagine the occasion and reconstruct the debate that took place there. Imagine this:

> *The King of France, Jean II, stung by the defeats inflicted on his father by the English, has brought together a great body of knights and constituted them as a royal chivalric order. He hopes to renew the practice of chivalry. So the king has them meet to discuss the law of arms, the principles, rules, and customs that they should live by. The king has chosen a famous knight, a man of practical experience and well-known eloquence, to lead the discussion. That knight, Sir Geoffroi de Charny, rises in his place, and with the aid of a list held by a secretary, begins to pepper the assemblage with a variety of questions, concerning jousting, tournaments, and warfare. He starts with easy queries about the basic rules of jousting, but soon is asking questions that would puzzle any assembly of schoolmen at the nearby University of Paris. Disagreement results, and soon the knights are heatedly debating questions about ransoms, on the division of booty, on whether a good knight can leave a battle and retain his renown. At last their leader calls a halt. They are far from unanimity, but they have had an education in how their fellow knights, all men of standing, understand their rights, duties, and obligations in the Year of Grace 1352. Their answers and their disagreements have provided all observers with a living encyclopedia of how knights understood chivalry and the life of "arms."*

If only we, too, had those answers.

The *Questions* as they exist for us do not constitute a written version of that imagined debate, which may indeed never have taken place. They are in fact simply questions that were meant to be presented to King Jean II of France and his Order of the Star. We don't know how they may have been used by the short-lived Order of the Star or how widely they may have been disseminated. Charny's authorship is secure; he is named as the proposer of the questions at the beginning of each of the three sections (on jousting, tournament, and war and each question is preceded by the phrase "Charny asks," or in a few cases, "I ask." The same thinking put forth in his other known works, *Charny's Book* (*Livre Charny*) and the *Book of Chivalry (Livre de chevalerie)*, is reflected in the *Questions.*

And of course, we have no answers (save for one marginal note in one manuscript), neither Charny's, nor King Jean's, nor anyone else's.[1] Not only do we have to imagine various scenarios to account for the existence of the *Questions*, we are equally dependent, in most cases, on imagination, logic, common sense, or speculation to suggest possible answers for the individual questions. Most scholars, perhaps sensibly, have shied away from doing so, or even from offering much in the way of analysis of the *Questions* as a whole. Unfortunately, this hesitation has led to a situation where the *Questions* are hardly known even to scholars. There is no easily available edition of the work, and the only translation is my own incomplete one of 2003, which includes the forty-one questions on jousts and tournaments, and only three of the ninety-three of those on war.[2]

If definitive answers about the practice of chivalry and the content of the law of arms are not provided, the *Questions* nevertheless do provide us something else of value—a picture of how knights, squires and other professional warriors of standing, "men-at-arms" in the terminology of Charny and his contemporaries, conceived of their way of life. It is a picture that is limited in scope—it does not by any means include everything we might like to know about such men—but has a tight and useful focus: on the ultimate activity that defined and justified the existence of "men-at-arms," the exercise of *armes*. Charny, provided with royal sponsorship and a pulpit in a prestigious forum, but also with an audience that was unlikely to be easily impressed, must have emphasized what both he and his listeners considered essential. He was presenting not simply his own concerns, and not just those which would meet the approval of his royal patron, but subjects which would speak to the identity and anxieties of his audience. However successful Charny's effort was, we cannot doubt his qualifications to lead such an effort. Indeed, Charny was very familiar with the people he addressed, and he must have been skilled in addressing them.

Charny is better known now than he was twenty years ago, thanks in large part to the efforts of Richard Kaeuper and Elspeth Kennedy; the facts of his life can be found in a number of places.[3] There is also no lack of good treatments of the Hundred Years War. However, the reader may appreciate a short introduction to Charny, his position in King Jean's regime, the task King Jean gave him, and the "law of arms" he discussed on the king's behalf.

Charny's Life and Career

Geoffroi de Charny was born before 1307 to a respectable if perhaps land-poor Burgundian family. He was a younger son, "a cadet of a cadet family,"[4] but one who could aspire to the rank of *chevalier* in an era when noble sons, even those who were active men-at-arms, often were content to be known as squires for their entire lives. Since Charny was the grandson of Jean de Joinville, the famous crusader and friend of King Louis IX (St. Louis), it is quite possible that Charny had opportunities that otherwise would have been unavailable—whether because of the reputation of his family, their financial support, or someone putting the right word in the right ear at the right time.

However it worked, Charny succeeded in building a successful career as a professional warrior of standing despite a start in life that great lords would have considered decidedly humble. He can be compared to a number of figures familiar from the pages of Froissart and fourteenth- and fifteenth-century chivalric biographies, men such as Boucicault the younger, Jean de Châteaumorand or Renaud de Roye, who as youngsters, moderately well-connected ones, raised their profiles by energetically throwing themselves into formal deeds of arms and by taking every opportunity to engage in warfare, adventure, and crusading expeditions.[5] Boucicault, for instance, the son of a marshal of France, enjoyed a certain amount of goodwill from the royal family, but had no close relative to keep watch over him after the early death of his father. He took it upon himself, therefore, to become the perfect man-at-arms, courageous, honed to physical perfection, and willing to go anywhere for a fight. This strategy worked, and eventually he too became a marshal of France, and a prominent player in the military and political establishment, despite what some modern observers might consider consistent bad luck and bad judgment in military affairs. Similar paths were followed by Châteaumorand and Roye, whose youthful exploits in arms not only opened doors to military careers of note, but also led them to be entrusted with significant diplomatic and political roles.

We have no details of Charny's accomplishments in the joust or in tourney, but nothing seems more likely than that he excelled in the lists. This is a man who in later life devoted part of each of his three books to praising these martial exercises as the proper preparation for a life in arms. Nevertheless, he considered them only an introduction to the serious business of warfare,[6] which Charny pursued as energetically as anyone of his time.

Charny began campaigning in Gascony, far from his home in Burgundy, in 1337, as soon as war broke out between the kings of England and France. Charny at this point was a *bachelier*, a term that in this case seems to indicate a yet-undubbed knight-aspirant. (It perhaps more commonly meant a knight who had no knights in his retinue, one who might follow a "knight banneret.") Despite being of good birth, he did not yet have the standing to claim the title of *chevalier*—perhaps because of lack of money and appropriate equipment.[7] Despite his limited financial resources, Charny excelled at war to the point that by 1342, at Morlaix in Brittany, he was granted command of the first line of cavalry. The French were defeated and Charny himself was captured and hauled off to England. It is unlikely that Charny had the funds to ransom himself, but someone provided him with money for that purpose, an indication that a powerful figure, despite the outcome of Morlaix, believed that Charny was a valuable military asset. At about the same time Charny was formally dubbed and began to be addressed as *chevalier*. Charny began to play a much bigger role in the French war effort. In 1342, straight out of captivity, he was appointed to the post of marshal in a French army operating in Brittany. In 1346, he took part in the successful defense of the town of Béthune, earning a mention in Froissart's *Chronicle*; because of his role in this siege he missed the battle of Crécy. When after Crecy the victorious King Edward turned his attention to besieging the channel port of Calais, Charny was part of King Philip's relieving force and was one of the men sent, in vain, to negotiate an agreement with the English to save the town. The other negotiators included two dukes and the Chancellor of France, which indicates how high Charny had climbed in the regard of the court and of men of affairs. For the rest of his life Charny not only served in the armies but was also deeply involved in political and diplomatic matters of the highest importance.[8]

He was most prominent as a military commander. By the time Philip VI mounted the aforementioned expedition to relieve Calais, in 1347, Charny was seen as a symbol of military virtue—he was given the office of holder of the Oriflamme, the sacred battle banner of France, which was brought out only for the most significant campaigns. Soon after the fall of the city, which made it a permanent and dangerous foothold for English forces, Charny was given command of the "marches of Calais and Flanders." Up until 1352, Charny more often than not was in charge of this region, which until the English invasions of 1356 remained the most important front in the war. It was a remarkable rise in his fortunes; this appointment could have been easily given to a royal prince.

During this period Charny's most remarkable military feat was a daring attempt to retake Calais by bribing its Lombard commander, Aimery de Pavia. In the late months of 1349, Charny found opportunity to offer a substantial bribe to this Italian man in English service. They agreed that Charny would pay Aimery 20,000 écus, "an enormous bribe" in Sumption's words,[9] which would be turned over when Charny himself showed up at the gates of the city in the middle of the night on the last day of the year. Unfortunately for Charny and his royal master, Aimery got cold feet, and when the French *chevalier* appeared to seal the deal, supported by a not-inconsiderable army,[10] he found himself facing a well-prepared English counterforce led by Edward III and Edward, Prince of Wales, who used the advantage of surprise to disperse the larger French force, killing perhaps two hundred French men-at-arms and capturing about thirty others, including Charny. A famous anecdote tells us that Edward treated his ranking prisoners graciously, but could not help singling out Charny for a chiding:

> *I rightly owe you very little love since you wanted to take from me by night what I have won and what has cost me much money: so I am very pleased to have you put to the test. You wanted to get it more cheaply than I, for 20,000 écus; but God aided me so that you failed in your intent. He will yet aid me, if it pleases Him, in my greater endeavor.*

Froissart, who tells the story, portrays Charny as standing in silence with "feelings of shame."[11]

Whatever the cause of that shame, Charny's reputation and standing in the French court did not suffer. Eventually, he was ransomed for 12,000 écus by no less than the new King of France, Jean II, who had succeeded to the throne in mid-1350. Within a year he had bailed Charny out[12] and granted him the title and responsibility of "Captain General of the Wars of Picardy in the Frontiers of Normandy."[13] King Jean would continue to entrust important responsibilities to Charny until Charny was killed by his side at Poitiers, still grasping the Oriflamme.

Here, then, is a short outline of the career of a very successful *chevalier* of the mid-fourteenth century—one who climbed to prominence through the traditional route of hard service in many wars. Charny however is known today for a different reason—as a philosopher of chivalry and the author of the *Book of Chivalry*. He is a unique witness—a practical, "strenuous" knight valued by his contemporaries for his judgment and determination and loyalty, who also recorded his thoughts on the life of the "man-at-arms," in other words a professional warrior of standing. Not only is his work eloquent—especially the *Book of Chivalry* translated by Elspeth Kennedy and edited by Richard Kaeuper—these writings allow us to reconstruct his own values and opinions, and place them in the context of King Jean's efforts to reform French chivalry and the relationship of the fighting nobility with the French crown. Indeed, we must look at this background to properly understand the significance of Charny's *Questions*.

Reform and the Order of the Star

During the first few decades of the Hundred Years War, the French royal cause suffered many defeats and gained very few victories.[14] Worse, most of the fighting between the two crowns took place within the kingdom of France. As a result, it was French territory, French cities, and French people which suffered from the raids and sieges that made up in military side of the war. Likewise it was the French crown that was usually seen, most of the time, as failing in its duty to protect its subjects, and its government as spending vast amounts of money irresponsibly and to little effect. The politically vocal segment of the French population was similarly critical of the failures of the nobility, whose legal privileges and social predominance had always been justified, and whose quick resort to private violence had always been excused, by their duty to defend the rest of society.[15] This dynamic played itself out in France over the entire period of the war; and though the political crisis that took place in the years after the battle of Crécy and the loss of Calais was less catastrophic than what was to come, the perceived loss of security was serious enough to bring down a storm of denunciation on the heads of the warrior class. At the same time, those warriors were not particularly happy with their own situation. The expenses and losses of those who fought during the 1340s were quite substantial, and they shared the general skepticism about Philip VI's leadership.[16]

When Philip's son Jean came to the throne after years of disorder, fiscal problems, and plague, quick and decisive action was required in a number of forums. Although Jean does not enjoy a high reputation for his judgment, especially his political judgment, he certainly was willing to take quick, even impulsive action, when he saw the need. And what he saw in regard to his military situation, besides the eternal need of war makers for more and more money, was the need to rally the fighting nobility around the throne, as his enemy Edward III was so successfully doing. In an effort to spark the kind of enthusiasm seen in English armies, Jean imitated a recent initiative of the English king, the establishment of a royal order of chivalry, the Order of the Garter, a corporate body made up of high-ranking lords and prominent professional soldiers (who would have been knights or lesser lords) whose loyalty and military pride was thereby focused on the leader of the company, the king himself. Founded around 1350 after a period of experimentation, the order was perhaps the most long-lived of Edward's many important innovations over a 50-year reign; the Garter still exists.

Something needs to be said about the concept of an "order of chivalry" and what medieval people meant when they designated a group as an order. Orders were the building blocks which made up society; an order had a defined place in the divine hierarchy, performed a necessary function, followed a worthy way of life. Used in this general sense, an order might be very large and rather diffuse. The order of chivalry discussed by Charny and some of his contemporaries ideally included all warriors of standing. The word order could also be used in a stricter sense to designate a body which attempted to realize the ideals of an order through corporate organization. Corporate orders might have a written rule of life, a carefully defined membership, administrative and religious officers and even considerable common property. Such corporate orders were usually reformist in nature. For instance, the Crusading chivalric orders, the Templars, the Hospitalers and so forth, were meant to harness the all too chaotic energy of knights by organizing and disciplining them on the model of the monastic orders. Members of these chivalric orders were in the view of their promoters and supporters a better kind of knight than the ordinary kind, fighting God's wars instead of persecuting their neighbors.

By the beginning of the fourteenth century, the Crusading movement had fallen into disarray and much of the shine had come off the Crusading orders. Yet the idea that the virtues of the overall order of chivalry could be harnessed for a worthy cause was not forgotten, it was simply picked up by kings. When kings began to found orders in the fourteenth century, they drew on a different, non-monastic and non-Crusading precedent. The subject of royal chivalric orders has been thoroughly studied by Boulton in his *Knights of the Crown*; the following account owes much to his research.

For a long time previously, since at least the mid-twelfth century, laypeople had been creating a culture where warriors and their associates set the standards. That chivalric culture had its own lore and rituals and explicit values, which were not those of the clergy. Much of that lay culture, the contemporary prominence of which was responsible for making the noun *chevalerie* mean more than a group of warriors on horseback, is lost to us. It was enacted in such rituals as dubbing (which recognized that a young man or, later, a particularly accomplished warrior, had attained a new status as *chevalier*) or distinctive collective activities like the tournament, rather than described in history or biography. However, an idealized construction of what it meant to be a worthy *chevalier* was available to contemporaries, as it is to us, in the form of epics and romances that showed the achievements of the legendary peers of Charlemagne and the knights of Arthur's Round Table. These denizens of story were known to every living knight, and served as examples of what a good and worthy knight did, whether while fighting the paynim, seeking adventures in distant and wild landscapes, or courting beautiful and inspiring ladies. Perhaps more relevant to us is the fact that they also showed groups of *chevaliers* acting and reacting to each other as brothers (not always loving brothers), living together a life that was difficult yet worthy of admiration. The knights of the Round Table, as seen in the near-infinite number of stories about Arthur's court, constituted a particularly influential picture of what chivalrous society should be like.[17]

Thus when Edward III sought a model on which to build a more chivalrous and glorious court, a court that would enthusiastically support his pretensions as a great conqueror, it was only natural that he should reach to the example of Arthur, the most famous monarch to rule Britain (and the successful conqueror of many other countries, including France). In the early part of his reign Edward, even when he was immersed in preparations for foreign wars, felt that there was no better way to increase the profile and reputation of his court than to sponsor elaborate tournaments—on a scale that no previous or later English king ever undertook.[18] A tournament-centered court was for him a chivalrous court, the proper setting for a great king. Eventually however, Edward seems to have become dissatisfied with patronizing a series of isolated tournaments and reached for something more permanent. What was Arthur—or the new Arthur—without a Round Table and a band of worthy knights to sit at it, when they were not actually pursuing adventures? In 1343, according to Froissart, Edward took the first steps towards creating what would eventually be the Order of the Garter, by publicly resolving to rebuild his birthplace, the castle at Windsor, and to establish his own Round Table in a huge building specifically created to house it.[19] According to the English chronicler Adam of Murimuth, the hall and the table were to be big enough to accommodate a company of three hundred knights.[20] The king threw himself into expensive preparations for this facility in 1344 and it is clear that he was serious about creating a headquarters for a permanent adjunct to English courtly life, a "confraternity of St. George" or "the knights of the blue garter."[21] Since Edward's plans were abandoned by the end of 1344, when the money being spent at Windsor had to be devoted to other uses, we can't be entirely sure how this company would have operated had it come to fruition. We do know, however, on the testimony of several chroniclers, that Edward's initial announcement came as the culmination of a series of magnificent tournaments,[22] that the announcement was celebrated by a tournament or joust, and the occasion was intended as a re-founding of the Round Table, or at least as a worthy prologue to it. Boulton says:

> *It is in fact quite possible that Edward intended the knights of his society to do no more than meet once a year for a great feast and tournament (perhaps of the "roundtable" variety [a type of tournament with an Arthurian theme]), for this is the only form of truly corporate activity attributed to the "original" society of the Round Table in any of the romances.*[23]

Even if his goals were limited to these, Edward's plan was an extraordinary one that speaks to great confidence on his part and the determination to make his court a wonder of the world.

Boulton believes that much of the inspiration for this early and abortive knightly order of England came from the prose romances of the time. He particularly draws our attention to the romance *Perceforest,* which depicted a company of pre-Arthurian knights, three hundred in number, who meet or live in a round tower called the *Franc Palais,* which housed an ivory table big enough to seat them all.[24] This detail among others speaks to the Arthurian inspiration of Edward III, but it is also relevant to the rival French initiative taken by Jean II not too long afterwards.

Very soon after the announcement of Edward's knightly order, and while he was still throwing huge resources into building its new headquarters at Windsor, Jean, the future king of France, was taking note and responding. He was perhaps concerned that Edward, who now claimed the French throne, might attract French members into his order, or simply that he, the heir of St. Louis, might be overshadowed. Letters written to Jean by Pope Clement VI in mid-1344 showed that the king had asked papal permission to create a church, staffed by priests and canons and dedicated to the Blessed Virgin and St. George, which would serve a congregation or communion of two hundred *chevaliers.* These *chevaliers* would gather at the church "not for jousts or tournaments or for any other act of arms, but for devotion to the same church"[25] on the Feast of the Assumption of the Blessed Virgin and the Feast of St. George. Thus it appears that Jean was countering Edward by proposing a more serious-minded congregation, rather than a glorified tournament-fighting society. A clear rivalry was indicated by Jean's imitative intention to assemble a very large number of knights who would gather around the (future) monarch in a headquarters built specially for the purpose. More than Edward's order with its explicit revival of the Round Table, Jean's congregation is reminiscent of the many other kinds of confraternities of pious laymen who gathered for spiritual purposes.[26]

Like Edward's proposed "confraternity of St. George," Jean's project went nowhere in the short term. We only need to think of the difficulties that the French royal regime was facing in the late 1340s and remember that Jean was not yet king at this time; even his status as heir to the throne was precarious. Once he succeeded in August 1350, it was not very long before he was, like Edward with the Garter, revising and re-structuring his original idea. We know what the new plan was, thanks to a surviving "letter of election," an archival model for the letters presumably sent to newly chosen members of the "Knights of Our Lady of the Noble House."[27] What the candidates were told by the king in such letters constitutes as much of a charter of the order as survives. For our purposes, the most important provisions are these: it was to be a large company, including five hundred knights. King Jean himself was to be the Prince, and this office would pass down to his royal successors. It was to be devoted to the Virgin Mary; the dedication to St. George was dropped because King Edward had already latched on to the warrior saint. The name of the order also emphasized the fact that it was to be given some permanence through the rebuilding of a royal estate at St. Ouen near Paris to be its headquarters. Unlike the confraternity-tournament company originally visualized by King Edward, Jean's foundation did not evoke specific Arthurian themes, but this idea of the community of worthy knights who gathered before their sponsor and benefactor, a king who built a home for them, would have spoken clearly to contemporaries. Indeed Jean Le Bel's account shows that the Flemish chronicler, at least, understood the company as having been ordained "at the example of the Round Table."[28]

It was an ambitious project for sure, as Boulton estimates the company "would have included between a fifth and an eighth of all the knights of the kingdom if Jean's plan had been completely implemented."[29] Jean's new company was meant to bring together *chevaliers* (a word in France sometimes used to indicate the entire fighting nobility, and not just those who were, in Jean's words, dubbed knights)[30] of all ranks—princes (i.e. great lords), bannerets (knights who could lead and support a retinue of other knights), and bachelors (knights without knightly followers of their own)—with the specific purpose of encouraging, in Jean's words, the "exultation of knighthood and the increase of honor."[31]

What did it mean to increase chivalry and honor? Jean was using his foundation to rededicate his noble warriors to effective warfare. The letter of election specifies that when the order met for its yearly assembly, nine worthy knights would be seated at a table of honor during the following dinner: three princes, three bannerets, and three bachelors. This no doubt was meant to evoke the symbolism of the Nine Worthies of chivalric legendry, the best knights of history.[32] The worthiness of the modern candidates was to be judged by their performance in *armes de guerre* in the preceding year. Jean wished this public praise to be based only on "knightly deeds performed on the field of battle, and explicitly excluded from consideration all *faits d'armes de paix* — feats that is to say, performed in tournaments and jousts." So, no doubt hoping to exploit the wide streak of pride in any warrior's makeup, the king also established that in each assembly the members were to recount their exploits "shameful as well as meritorious" so they could be written down as a permanent record in a special book — an idea taken from romance literature.[33] A final point is that, according to Jean le Bel's *Chronicle*, "they were to swear that they would never flee in battle or farther than four *arpents* (in their opinion) but would die or surrender."[34]

It is clear just from what we have seen that the Order of the Star (as it became known from its badge[35]) was part of a reform initiative to restore the fighting capabilities of his kingdom. We will look in a moment at the king's revamping of army pay and command structures, an important practical initiative. The company or order, however, was a sweeping ideological effort to infuse the spirit of *chevalerie* into the *chevalerie* of France, that is, into those who by rank and descent should already be characterized by chivalric virtue. The foundation of the order was part of an effort to meet what was perhaps the king's greatest challenge. Jean defined this challenge in 1352, when he restated his goals for the Order of the Star in letters creating a body of clergy associated with the order. In the preamble of this letter, the king stated the reasons he was dissatisfied with the fighting nobility and his hopes for their improvement:

> *...after many long centuries [of martial success], some of the members of this order [of knighthood] unaccustomed to arms and deprived of exercises, or for some other cause unknown to us, have immoderately plunged themselves into the idleness and vanity [of] the age, to the contempt of honor, alas, and of their own good renown, to diminish their gaiety of heart in exchange for the comfort of their persons.*
>
> *For this reason we, mindful of former times... have taken it to heart to recall the same liegemen, present and future, to a perfect union, to the end that in this intimate unity they will breathe nothing but honor and glory, renouncing the frivolities of inaction, and will, through respect for the prestige and nobility of knighthood, restore to our epoch the luster of their ancient renown and of their illustrious company, and that after they have brought about the reflowering of the honor of knighthood through the protection of divine goodness, a tranquil peace will be reborn for our reign and our subjects, and the praises of their virtue will be published everywhere... and we affirm confidence... that the same knights, eager for honor and glory in the exercise of arms shall bear themselves with such concord and valiance, that the flower of chivalry, which for a time and for the reasons mentioned had faded into the shadows, shall blossom in our realm, and shine resplendent in a perfect harmony to the honor and glory of the kingdom and of our faithful subjects.*[36]

As Boulton says, "the complaints and criticism expressed here are essentially similar to those voiced by Jean and the other critics of the knights of France in 1347 (and indeed by the critics of contemporary knighthood throughout the period)."[37]

King Jean had a further purpose than moral rearmament in creating this order. The resulting order would have been very large and made up of wealthy and experienced warriors and men of affairs. Jean saw the potential for the order to be an advisory or legislative body, the sort that did not exist mid-fourteenth century France. The Estates General were rarely and reluctantly called by the royal government, and only in times of great crisis. The Star however was meant to be gathered together annually for purposes we have already seen, and the additional purpose of being available to advise the king on a variety of issues. Item 8 of the letter of election says specifically: "They shall swear that according to their ability they will give loyal counsel to the prince concerning anything he asks, either about arms or other things."[38]

Having seen King Jean's goals and how the Star was meant to promote them, it is time to note that Geoffroi de Charny likely wrote his three works when these same ideas were in the air. These three consist of his verse contemplation on the life of arms, *Charny's Book;* his more extensive prose treatise, *The Book of Chivalry;* and the document we are most concerned with here, the *Questions*. Except for the *Questions*, which clearly states that it is associated with the Order of the Star, we have no indication of when Charny decided to write about issues of chivalry and the life of arms. However, the similarities in outlook among the three works and with the expressed concerns of Charny's patron make it difficult to doubt that Charny's other two books, *Charny's Book* and the *Book of Chivalry,* were a product of the same effort that produced the Star.

The Order of the Star did not survive very long. The founding meeting of the members, then newly appointed, took place on the eve of the Epiphany in January of 1352—as we shall see an important event in our understanding of Charny's *Questions*. Boulton shows us, however, that the letter of election called for the regular meetings of the company to be held on the feast of the Assumption in August. The first of these regular conclaves, which was to have taken place in 1352, never met. During that summer, according to Jean Le Bel and Froissart, a good many Knights of the Star were taking part in resisting an English invasion of Brittany. The day before the meeting of the order should have taken place, what was perhaps a majority of its members took part in the battle of Mauron in Brittany. Acting on the newly reaffirmed obligation to act more courageously than the French army had at Crécy, these knights were killed to a number of eighty-nine. According to Le Bel the oath of the order led to this catastrophe:

> *...they had sworn they would never flee; for if it not been for the oath they could well have withdrawn. Several others died for the love of them, who might have been saved if they had not sworn the oath, and feared that they would be reproved for it by the Company.*[39]

This tremendous blood-letting of the membership left Jean's plans for the order in disarray. He had little opportunity to revive it before the defeat at Poitiers, even less so afterwards when myriad problems needed to be dealt with. Left behind, though, were Charny's *Questions,* which throws some light not only on Charny as a theorist of the life chivalry, but on the man he served, and on the warriors to whom the king entrusted his project of chivalric reform. In the next chapter we will examine Charny's literary labors in aid of that project.

Endnotes

1. There are two editions of Charny's Questions in unpublished dissertations: Jean Rossbach, "Les Demandes pour la joute, le tournoi, et la guerre de Geoffroy de Charny (XIVème siècle)," (diss. Université libre de Bruxelles, 1961–2); Michael Anthony Taylor, ed. "A Critical Edition of Geoffroy de Charny's 'Livre Charny' and the 'Demandes pour la joute, les tournois, et la guerre.' " Unpublished Ph.D. dissertation, (University of North Carolina, 1977). Neither attempted an extensive analysis of the law of arms.
2. *Jousts and Tournaments: Charny and the rules for chivalric sport in fourteenth-century France* (Union City, CA: Chivalry Bookshelf, 2002).
3. The fullest scholarly treatment is in Richard W. Kaeuper and Elspeth Kennedy, *The Book of Chivalry of Geoffroi de Charny: Text, Context, and Translation* (Philadelphia: University of Pennsylvania Press, 1996). See also Philippe Contamine, "*Geoffroy de Charny (début de XIVe siècle-1356), 'Le plus prudhomme et le plus vaillant de tous les autres,'* " *Histoire et société: mélanges offerts à Georges Duby.* 2 vols. (Aix-en-Provence: Université de Provence, 1992) 2:107–21. For Charny in context, Jonathan Sumption's, *The Hundred Years War,* vol. 2, *Trial by Fire* (Philadelphia: University of Pennsylvania Press, 1999), 2:12, 60–2, 9–3, 98, 238, 247.
4. Contamine, as quoted by Kaeuper and Kennedy, 3.
5. Steven Muhlberger, *Deeds of Arms: Formal Combats in the Late Fourteenth Century* (Highland Village TX: Chivalry Bookshelf, 2005), 155–185.
6. Kaeuper and Kennedy, 84–7.
7. Kaeuper and Kennedy, 5–6.
8. It is suggestive that Charny was named to the royal council as a new member whose inclusion might placate criticism from the Estates General in 1347. Likewise in 1354 and 1355 he was sent to negotiate with the scheming royal cousin Charles the Bad, King of Navarre, very touchy diplomatic missions that involved the bitter internal politics of the French dynasty. Kaeuper and Kennedy, 9; Sumption, 2:125, 165–6.
9. Sumption, 2:60.
10. Sumption 2:61; contemporaries estimated the force at 1500 men-at-arms and 4000 infantry.
11. Kaeuper and Kennedy, 12, citing Froissart, 5:250.
12. What may seem to be a substantial delay in Jean acting on Charny is probably only an indication of how full the King's hands were. D'Arcy Jonathan Dacre Boulton, *The Knights of the Crown: The Monarchical Orders of Knighthood in Later Medieval Europe 1325–1520* (Woodbridge: Boydell Press, 2000), 177.
13. Kaeuper and Kennedy, 13.
14. For its context in the greater war, Sumption, 2:33–5.
15. Georges Duby, *The Three Orders: Feudal Society Imagined* (Chicago: University of Chicago Press, 1982).
16. Sumption, 2:46.
17. Boulton, 23–4, 93–4, 107–11; Richard W. Kaeuper, *Holy Warriors: The Religious Ideology of Chivalry* (Philadelphia: University of Pennsylvania Press, 2009), 155–9..
18. Boulton, 101; David Crouch, *Tournament* (London: Hambledon and London, 2005), 130.
19. Boulton, 105–7.
20. Boulton, 104–5.
21. Boulton, 102.
22. Boulton, 104.
23. Boulton, 108.
24. Boulton, 23.
25. Boulton, 175.
26. Boulton, 175–7.
27. Boulton, 178.
28. Boulton, 180.

29. Boulton, 190.
30. Boulton 170–1.
31. Boulton, 178.
32. Maurice Keen, *Chivalry* (New Haven: Yale University Press, 1984), 121–4.
33. Boulton, 200.
34. Boulton, 181.
35. Boulton, 201–5; the badge was also a reference to the Virgin as "star of the sea."
36. Boulton, 184–5, translating an archival document from October 1352 Paris, AN, Reg JJ 81, no. 570, f. 288r.
37. Boulton, 185.
38. Boulton, 194, and n. 81.
39. Boulton, 182, translating *Chronique de Jean le Bel*, ed. Jules Viard and Eugène Déprez. 2 vols. (Paris: Renouard, 1906), 206–7.

2 CHARNY'S QUESTIONS ON JOUSTS, TOURNAMENT, AND WAR

Charny: Writer on Chivalry

Charny's three works on the life of arms make him a person of unusual significance for our understanding of French military society around 1350. The list of medieval warriors who wrote on this subject is a short one; it is hard to identify one with significant martial experience who, like Charny, wrote as much as he. For historians interested in military affairs and chivalry, his three works constitute a small but valuable trove of material reflecting one insider's view of the life of arms.

Perhaps the first of the three is the *Livre Charny* (*Charny's Book*); that title would be unambiguous only if Charny had not yet written anything else. Both *Charny's Book* (written in verse) and the *Book of Chivalry* (in prose) are devoted to describing the challenges and the rewards of the professional warrior's life. It seems likely that the prose work is a more developed version of the earlier poem.

Charny's *Questions* spells out its relationship to the Order of the Star in its very first lines:

> *These are the questions concerning the joust which I, Geoffroi de Charny, pose to the high and mighty prince of the Knights of Our Lady of the Noble House to be judged by you and the knights of our noble company.*

The other two sections of the *Questions,* on the tournament and war, are introduced in almost exactly the same words. These prologues state that the order as a group will advise the king on the issues laid out in them—just as the king had visualized in his letter of election. While *Charny's Book* and the *Book of Chivalry* do not mention the Order of the Star, they are connected to each other and to the *Questions* by thematic structure. The *Questions'* division of the warrior's life into three categories, jousting, tourneying, and war, is used as an organizing principle in all three works. Charny's description of the same "scale of prowess"[1] from least dangerous (jousting) to most dangerous (war) lies behind his lengthy introductory passages in the other two works.[2] The moral and practical themes that Charny treats in *Charny's Book* and the *Book of Chivalry* are also related, and reflect the stated concerns of the King. Not only are all three of Charny's writings concerned with many of the same problems, the approach to solving those problems is the same. Charny consistently argues that the life of arms is a difficult one but perhaps the most honorable of all; those who wish to win honor and do their duty to God in this profession could do so by following a simple rule: "he who does more is of greater worth [*Qui plus fait, miex vault*],"[3] a "key idea"[4] Charny repeats in various forms in all three works. Thus, all scholars who have looked closely at the material have leaned toward the conclusion that royal initiative was the impetus behind Charny's writings. Likewise, it is generally assumed that they were written in the very late 1340s or the early 1350s, during Charny's captivity in England, or after his return when Jean was planning and implementing his military reforms.

Charny and Chivalry

Geoffroi de Charny wrote a book entitled *The Book of Chivalry,* which makes it difficult to avoid the conclusion that he was a professor and follower of chivalry, that he set out first and foremost to praise, to define, and to teach chivalry. No doubt; yet most of us come to Charny with a pretty clear idea of what we mean by chivalry, and unconsciously tend to substitute our meaning for the various meanings detectable in the works of Charny and other chivalric reformers. We sometimes also tend to ignore the fact that "chivalry" is often absent from texts or discourses where we might expect to find it.[5]

Thus, if we look at Charny very carefully and try to find what he means by chivalry, and when he feels the need to invoke it, and when he does not, we notice a number of things. First, Charny uses the words *chevalerie* ("chivalry") and *chevalier* ("knight") much less frequently than we might suppose. Even in the *Book of Chivalry,* the word *chevalerie* is used only in two sections: the first is in his discussion of the virtues of the ancient military leaders Julius Caesar and Judas Maccabeus, who are praised primarily for their *preudomie* (honesty, integrity), for being "men of [supreme] worth."[6] Charny gives these two great examples what for him is a rare accolade, being referred to not as men-at-arms but as *chevaliers;* each indeed is called *tres bon chevalier.* Second, in the section where Charny describes the idealized ceremony of dubbing for making a knight (which description he borrowed from the thirteenth-century text *L'Ordene de Chevalerie*) he again writes of *chevaliers,* and even *l'orde de chevalerie.*[7] We find no mention of an abstract *chevalerie* in *Charny's Book,* and only three offhand uses of *chevalier.* In the *Questions, chevaliers* are discussed in some contexts, but the word *chevalerie* is not present. This is curious at first encounter, but is not the product of this knightly author's disdain for the concept or the word. He uses it, along with *preudomie* and *vaillance,* to indicate the highest and most honorable level of martial achievement. Then why doesn't it appear? *Chevalerie* was a word too likely to be associated only with dubbed knights, *chevaliers,* those who bore the title *sire* or *messire.* What Charny says in his book is not meant solely for knights or would-be knights; a subject we shall return to later. He used more inclusive language, preferring to speak of men in *armes* or about the *mestier d'armes,* "the life of arms."

Despite this perhaps initially confusing terminology, Charny's works tell us what he thought about the great issues raised by King Jean's effort to exalt knighthood and increase honor[8] and what his readers presumably needed to know. Charny spoke about the life of arms out of a deep conviction that such a way of life was exceedingly worthy when properly practiced (an idea not absent from Ramon Llull, an earlier writer on chivalric reform). It was perhaps the most worthy of all possible professions: although he speaks of the order of priesthood as being "the worthiest order of all,"[9] he then designates the order of knighthood (*ordre de chevalerie*) as "the most rigorous order of all, especially for those who uphold it well and conduct themselves in the manner in keeping with the purpose for which the order was established."[10] He compares that order in *Charny's Book* with martyrdom.[11] Because of the physical and spiritual challenges that men-at-arms face,

> *...one can only well say truly that of all the men in the world, of whatever estate, whether religious or lay, none have as great a need to be a good Christian to the highest degree or to have such true devoutness in their hearts nor to lead a life of such integrity and to carry out all their undertakings loyally and with good judgment as do these good men-at-arms who have the will to pursue this calling as has been set out above wisely and according to God's will. For there is in such men no firm purpose to cling to life; they should rather show firmness in the face of death and be prepared to meet it at any time.*[12]

As Kaeuper points out, "there can be no thought that a life of fighting counts against the man-at-arms. Some say a man cannot save his soul through fighting, Charny assures his audience that they can save or lose their souls in any profession.... Those who fight well but die in the fray need not fear; they will be taken into God's select company to enjoy paradise forever."[13]

The worthiness of this order of society is in the difficulties that a good man-at-arms faces; and having convinced himself years earlier that this is the case, Charny is more concerned about those faults and distractions that pull men away from this life, than with the abuses of power inherent in fighting.

Taking a stand of respect towards all good men-at-arms, and believing "there are no small feats of arms, but only great and good ones,"[14] he does not excoriate those whose performance may not be perfect, such as those who are brave but too eager for plunder. This can be a great fault: "It often occurs that through lack of those who chase after plunder before the battle is over, that which is thought to be already won can be lost again and lives and reputations as well." But he continues: "And yet one should praise and value those men-at-arms who are able to make war on, inflict damage on, and profit from their enemies, for they cannot do it without strenuous effort and great courage. But again I shall repeat: he who does best is most worthy."[15]

The faults he most energetically denounces are those of the frivolous, the lazy, the fearful, and the degenerate, those who throw themselves into playing games of real tennis, or dice, which should be left to "rakes, bawds, and tavern rogues."[16] Even worse, if we are to judge by his tone, are those who dress indecently. Worst of all are those guilty of laxness in the unwillingness to take any risks, and therefore avoid their proper role:

> *...these wretched people are so afraid of dying that they cannot overcome their fear. As soon as they leave their abode, if they see a stone jutting off the wall a little further than the others, they will never dare to pass beneath it, for it would always seem to them that it would fall on their heads. If they come to a river which is a little big or too fast flowing, it always seems to them, so great is their fear of dying, that they will fall into it. If they cross a bridge which may seem a little too high or too low, they dismount and are still terrified lest the bridge collapse under them, so great is their fear of dying... Now you can see that these wretched people who are so fainthearted will never feel secure from living in greater fear and dread of losing their lives than do those good men-at-arms who have exposed themselves to so many physical dangers and perilous adventures in order to achieve honor; for they are so accustomed to and familiar with such things that they are quite unaffected by such pathetic fears to which these wretches are so often subject. And while the cowards have a great desire to live and a great fear of dying, it is quite the contrary for the men of worth who do not mind whether they live or die, provided that their life be good enough for them to die with honor.*[17]

It is clear what kind of man Charny believes to be the most worthy; not those who require soft beds, but:

> *those who have the will to achieve great worth [who] because of their great desire to reach and attain that high honor ... do not care what suffering they have to endure, but turn everything into great enjoyment. Indeed, it is a fine thing to perform great deeds, for those who rise to great achievement cannot rightly grow tired or sated with it; so the more they achieve, the less they feel they have achieved; this stems from the delight they take in striving constantly to reach greater heights. And great good comes from performing these deeds, for the more one does, the less one is proud of oneself, and it always seems that there is so much left to do.*[18]

The importance of this statement and others like it can be seen when we return to King Jean's letter of October 1352 and read again his characterization of "this order"[19] having become "unaccustomed to arms and deprived of exercises, or from other cause unknown to us, have immoderately plunged themselves into the idleness and vanity of the contempt of honor, alas, of their good renown..." Charny may not have given us a precise definition of *chevalerie*, but we can be quite sure what military virtues he prized most highly.

The Law of Arms, the Laws of War, and Charny's *Questions*

What is the law of arms?

The best treatment is still Maurice Keen's *The Laws of War in the Late Middle Ages*,[20] which argues for the development in the fourteenth and fifteenth centuries of a systematic and reasonably enforceable international law applicable to all men-at-arms, one of the roots of the law of war in later centuries. Keen emphasized two major influences on the late medieval evolution of military law. The first was the theoretical framework which related the law of arms to Roman civil law, canon law, the law of nations and natural and divine law, a framework which saw considerable development from the later fourteenth century, as scholars sought to provide some kind of legal method to mitigate the effects of wide-ranging war throughout Western Europe. This theoretical work sought to bring the resolution of disputes related to war into line with the logic of positive law which already existed in an established tradition. Keen argued that this was done by considering the law of arms (note: not war) as a professional law of the knightly warriors, who could be considered as the legal equivalent of the Roman soldier. This theoretical work, however, did not start from scratch. Keen believed that practical soldiers considered the law of arms not as a professional law, but as the law of a certain privileged class—their own—whose hereditary occupation was fighting. He argued that these two legal traditions, one emphasizing logical rigor, the other establishing practice, came together starting about the time Charny wrote.[21]

Charny's *Questions*, which do not express any explicit theoretical stance, appear to be the best example of what established practice and soldierly opinion looked like just before canon lawyers began to try to reduce their customary law to a branch of the law of nations. To illustrate this point, it will be useful to briefly examine some documents that typify both learned and customary law, so that we can appreciate the unique aspects of the *Questions*.

Disciplinary Ordinances

The law of arms may perhaps best be seen as a broad framework that takes in generally accepted principles, as opposed to ordinances meant to regulate a specific situation. Ordinances were the legislation of a prince or those delegated part of his jurisdiction, who included commanders of armies, to meet particular disciplinary needs. We have a number of military ordinances or fragments of them stretching from the twelfth century to the fifteenth (and of course beyond). Such ordinances of arms that we have were primarily meant to keep order in a military camp. Summaries of two such documents survive in chronicles from the twelfth century. Both chronicles are describing crusading armies: the mostly English armies that attacked Lisbon in 1147, and the multinational army Richard Lionheart led during the Third Crusade. What survives of the Lisbon ordinances features articles on restraining disorder and sinful behavior in the fleet, in an effort to make sure the army not only retained its discipline but also remained pleasing to God:

> *Among these people of so many different tongues the firmest guarantees of peace and friendship were taken; and, furthermore, they sanctioned very strict laws, as for example a life for a life and a tooth for a tooth. They forbade all display of costly garments. Also they ordained that women should not go out in public; that the peace must be kept by all, unless they should suffer injuries recognized by the proclamation; that weekly chapters be held by the laity and clergy separately, unless perchance some great emergency should require their meeting together; that each ship should have its own priests and keep the same observances as are prescribed for parishes; that no one retain the seaman or the servant of another in his employ; that every one make weekly confession and take communion on Sunday; and so on through the rest of the obligatory articles with separate sanctions for each.*[22]

Richard Lionheart's Crusading ordinances of 1190 show similar concerns:

> *Richard the grace of God [etc.] Know ye that we by the common counsel of fit and proper men, have made the enactments written below.*
>
> *Whoever shall slay a man on shipboard shall be bound to the dead man and thrown into the sea. If he shall slay him on land, he shall be bound to the dead man and buried in the earth. If anyone shall be convicted, by means of lawful witnesses, of having drawn a knife with which to strike another, or shall strike another so as to draw blood, he shall lose his hand. And if he shall strike a blow of his hand, without shedding blood, he shall be plunged in the sea three times. If anyone shall utter disgraceful language or abuse, or shall curse his companion, he shall pay an ounce of silver for every time he has so abused him. A robber who is convicted of theft shall have to his head cropped like that of a hired fighter, and boiling pitch shall be poured over it, and then the feathers of a cushion shall be shaken out upon him, so that he may be known, and as soon as the ships touch land shall be put ashore...*[23]

Certainly such ordinances were not invented in the twelfth century; these are simply the ones that were preserved because of widespread interest in the conduct of Crusading armies. Nor were ordinances only concerned with the moral tone of the camp. The thirteenth-century English chronicler Matthew Paris tells a story about an Anglo-French conflict in St. Louis' crusading army which involved disciplinary regulations. The Englishman William Longespee secretly took his forces out on a successful plundering raid, to meet on his return fierce resentment from the French members of the same army, who were hungry:

> *The French, who had remained inactive and were in great want, stimulated by feelings of envy and avarice, met him, on his arrival, in a hostile way, and, like daring robbers, forcibly took from him all that he had gained, imputing it to him as a sufficient fault, that, in his rash presumption, contrary to the king's order, and the ordinances of the chiefs of the army, and also to military discipline, he had proudly and foolishly separated from the whole body of the army. When William heard this, he promised to give them satisfaction in every way, by allowing all the food that he had obtained to be distributed amongst the needy army; but the French cried out against this, claimed it all for themselves, and seized on all of it immediately; thus adding insult to injury. William, therefore, grieved in bitterness of spirit at suffering such an injury, made a heavy complaint to the king in the matter... the count of Artois arrived, excited and furious, like a madman, and, without saluting the king, or those sitting round, he raised his voice, and exclaimed in great anger: "What does this mean, my lord king? Do you presume to defend this Englishman, and to oppose your own Frenchmen? This man, in contempt of you and the whole army, urged by his own impetuosity, has of his own accord clandestinely carried off booty by night, contrary to our decrees; and owing to this, the fame of him alone, and not of the French king or his people, has spread through all the provinces of the East; he has obscured all our names and titles."*[24]

It is hard to visualize any effective army in any era which did not have some kind of rules, but we have no complete examples before Charny's time.[25] Furthermore, ordinances were not part of a permanent body of legislation. Each individual set of ordinances was issued for a given campaign. Richard II issued multiple ordinances, as did Henry V. Any given ordinance might express practices springing from the law of arms, but it was not a compilation or a systematic survey of the law of arms; nor were these regulations drawn from a learned tradition. Charny's *Questions* refer to such ordinances in connection with the division of booty (W49, 53, 55) but otherwise say nothing about them.[26]

Administrative Ordinances

Regulation of a different sort can be found in King Jean's ordinance of April 30, 1351, the *Reglement pour le gens de guerre,*[27] which we have mentioned before. This detailed and practical document does not overlap significantly with such disciplinary ordinances such as Richard II's or Henry V's. Rather, it is a recruiting document and a financial and administrative guideline. The prologue of the *Reglement* begins by admitting that the customary pay offered to both *gens d'armes* (mounted, armored warriors) and the footmen (*gens de pié*) have been inadequate. It goes on to specify (in paragraph 1) a new and augmented pay scale for bannerets, chevaliers, esquires, armed valets and later on (in paragraph 8) for footmen; the tone is almost that of a friendly advertisement, and the *Reglement* certainly is an attempt to attract and recruit an army of suitable warriors, of specified types and—important point—specified equipment. The rest of the *Reglement* outlines an administrative arrangement which tells not only potential recruits but also the royal officials who command and organize armies who is qualified to receive wages. It also describes the mustering procedure that will assure the king's accountants and generals that the men they are paying for are actually present in the military units that they have been assigned to, and are properly equipped to do their assigned duties.

The *Reglement pour le gens de guerre* is a pioneering document in French royal practice and of especial interest to us as an indication of what was happening in the royal court in the period of Jean's reform efforts, but it is hardly unique. Northern European administrative adaptation to the need to raise armies through wages had been preceded by Italian efforts in the same direction. Italian republics were often at war and in the thirteenth and fourteenth century relied increasingly on mercenary armies. For a variety of reasons Italian governments had to be very careful about lines of authority, financial management, and so forth, so we see a number of similar and earlier documents in the peninsula.[28]

Such ordinances, like the army ordinances, are specific enactments intended for a limited time and for a specific sphere of operation. They could be amended at any time by the issuing authority. Further, an ordinance issued by an Italian republic had no force in France or England, and theirs would have no force in Italy. Various ordinances or individual enactments might serve as an example or precedent for another legislation or elsewhere, but they were not of themselves the kind of international law discussed by Keen.

Theoretical Treatises on War

In the late thirteenth and fourteenth century we begin to find wider and more theoretical treatments on the legalities of warfare: Beaumanoir's famous customary for the French province of the Beauvaisis (1283) contains a section on how *guerre* was regulated in a regional context.[29] Beaumanoir's war was limited conflict among noble or gentle warriors, backed by members of their lineages. For such people who had the privilege of waging war, it was an alternative method of dispute settlement in place of appeal to a superior lord. This kind of *guerre* (in modern times called "private war") was a subset of the *guerre* treated in the third section of Charny's *Questions*, and Beaumanoir was concerned entirely with who enjoyed that privilege and how they were permitted to exercise it. Charny discusses such warfare between neighbors and lineages in four or five of his ninety-three questions on war (W12, 20, 22, 23 and perhaps 73). Most of the legal problems he proposes, however, concern what seem to be larger, more extensive wars that often involve "captains of countries" and sometimes foreign knights and their retinues. Most of the issues Charny discusses are not referred to at all by Beaumanoir.

If the wide-ranging wars of the fourteenth century were going to have a law of their own, it would have to be based on something broader than local privilege in one county or duchy or even a given kingdom. Legal disputes concerning war became so common in the mid-fourteenth century, and so often involved litigation between warriors of different countries, that professional systematizers, university-trained lawyers, began to tackle the problem. The first textual product of this effort was an Italian work, Giovanni da Legnano's *Treatise on War Reprisals and Duels* (1360).[30] It was followed about a generation later by a French translation and adaptation by Honoré Bouvet, *The Tree of Battles* (1387).[31] Both works sought to bring together in a single treatise all the relevant laws and precedents on the proper and legitimate waging of war. Both men lived in war-torn countries, so this was not merely an academic exercise; both no doubt hoped to influence actual practice. Legnano, who as a "doctor of both laws" (civil and canon) and therefore the possessor of sterling formal qualifications, was also an active participant in the complex and unstable politics of Bologna (at whose university he taught and wrote), Italy, and the papacy. From 1377 until shortly before his death in 1382, he was papal vicar in Bologna, which made him perhaps the most powerful official resident in the city.[32] In the case of Bouvet, the author is explicit in his aims. A proper understanding of war might lead to peace among Christians, who, under the leadership of the King of France, could work together to defend Christendom from its enemies.[33] To create an intellectual framework for this ambitious project, he devoted a long introductory section to define war and to discuss its history from the time of the better angels' war against Lucifer until more recent times—the reign of Augustus. When he proceeded in books three and four to discuss the content of the laws of war, he relied primarily on Justinian's code, the decretals of canon law and Giovanni da Legnano's interpretations of those sources. Bouvet on rare occasions cited the current usage by soldiers, which he in general had little respect for. Current usage by soldiers was one of the problems the two lawyers sought to correct.

Both lawyers used the common academic method of posing questions and providing answers based on both logic and precedent. As was often the case in such scholastic works, the questions were far-ranging: Bouvet treated the theological and legal theory of war ("whether it is possible in the nature of things that the world should be at peace;" "from what law does war come?"), the characteristics of a good warrior ("what constitutes boldness in a knight?"); and many other issues, in particular focusing on who can "ordain" war—legitimately wage it—and what rights and duties combatants and noncombatants alike had in war. It is the use of questions to explore the boundaries of the subject matter that is the most important similarity between these men's work and Charny's *Questions on War.*

There are important differences, too. For Bouvet and Giovanni da Legnano, limitations on violence were a key issue. Both were seeking to construct public order using the discipline that they had been trained in. They were both particularly interested in restricting the right to wage war to appropriate authorities. These treatises are not entirely devoted to legal theory and hypothetical cases ("whether a man may take arms to defend his wife without license of court")[34], or very large questions about the moral structure of the universe, but also include questions of immediate import to actual warriors. When Bouvet treats the case of whether a captive sworn to obey his "master" (captor) can legitimately escape his mistrusting captor if he has shut him up in a strong prison, the lawyer begins by saying "I have often heard the following case discussed among nobles."[35]

Charny's *Questions*

Thus we see that Charny was hardly alone in discussing, or seeking to discuss, how law could or should regulate the waging of war. Putting such material in written form was not new in his time. During the later Middle Ages and even before, a variety of different aspects of war were treated at length in legal treatises, administrative documents, and ordinances to control the behavior of warriors and hangers-on in military camps. Yet none of the works we have surveyed are closely related to Charny's *Questions*, and the implied view of law found in Charny's discussion is not represented in them. To put it simply, the other writers are not discussing or working within what Charny called the "*droit d'armes.*"[36] With a few minor exceptions, the phrase is missing. Giovanni da Legnano speaks of *bellum*, Bouvet (and King Jean) about *guerre.*

This terminological difference is reflected in the distinctiveness of the material treated by Charny in his questions. First let us look at the many subjects included elsewhere that Charny omits. He says nothing about enforcing religious obligation and rectitude, although Charny himself was far from indifferent to religion. Charny's *Questions* do not discuss pay rates, armoring standards, the size of military units, or the use of musters to enforce regulation of such matters. He barely touches on the question of disorder in the camp, the (quite understandable) emphasis of various royal ordinances of war. Likewise Charny seems uninterested in discussing discipline in the sense of obeying orders, or the duty of good men-at-arms to serve in the army in the first place. Most importantly, Charny does not care to place the issues of the law of arms in any kind of learned theoretical legal context. The fate, the duties, and the rights of noncombatants, discussed in a number of questions in Bouvet's and Giovanni da Legnano's legal treatises, are missing from his work.[37] Nor do any of the other writers show any interest in what the law of arms had to say about jousting and tournaments.

The only subjects where there is significant overlap between Charny's concerns and the concerns of other writers are regulation of ransom in captivity and the division of loot, a commonality worth looking at in more detail later. Otherwise Charny is looking at other issues, expressing or probing a different tradition from the others. Nicholas Wright has defined it thus:

> *The law of arms regulated the day-to-day conduct of men-at-arms and was based upon the customs and traditions of their profession... The matter of the law of arms was drawn almost entirely from the areas of potential dispute between men-at-arms concerning the taking of knightly prisoners, the ransoms which could be demanded of them, the distribution of the profits of war between companions in arms, the organization of tournaments and jousts, coats of arms, loss and gain of reputation... It was... a professional code of knightly soldiers with no points of reference outside that noble group.*[38]

Wright's description of "the matter of the law of arms" could hardly be better as a brief description of what we find in Charny's *Questions*—indeed it evidently was influenced by Wright's own reading of the *Questions*.[39] One might only wish to add what Keen believed was a significant difference between the attitudes of civilian and canon lawyers on one hand and warriors[40] on the other:

> *For the soldier...* jus militare *did not so much mean a professional law, as the law of a certain privileged class, whose hereditary occupation was fighting.*[41]

The *Questions* reveal the knights Charny wished to interrogate primarily as a professional group keenly aware of their personal privileges and the common knightly interest, to the exclusion of almost everything else. We cannot say that Charny was indifferent to the effects of war on non-combatants; he has a whole section in *The Book of Chivalry* on the obligation of emperors, kings and princes, whom he sees as knights writ large, to provide good government.[42] And in another place he condemns "cowards and traitors" who "attack anyone, taking booty, prisoners and other valuables, if they find them, and without justification."[43] But those issues are not explored in the *Questions*. Instead, that work addresses the man-at-arms as military practitioner, who was expected to be familiar with the customs that governed his profession, and in particular those customs which regulated his relationship with other men-at-arms. Matters that did not impact quite so directly on the individual man-at-arms were often skimped or ignored altogether.

Readers familiar with Charny will recall that he set himself up in some sections of the *Book of Chivalry* as an arbiter of appropriate behavior—in love, in dress, in the kind of amusements that men-at-arms might pursue in peacetime—and we can see him taking a similar stance in the *Questions*. The inclusion of questions about the law of arms for jousts and tourneys points to an important feature of his worldview and his writing project. Charny was trying to promote, maybe even revive, traditional activities that were no longer so central, at least in their established forms, to both the training of warriors and noble identity.[44] Charny was acting as a champion of a threatened chivalric culture, and though knowledge and practice of the law of arms was part of what he wished to restore, even in the *Questions* he had more than a merely military view of the proper role of "men-at-arms."

What was the Purpose of Charny's *Questions*?

The exact purpose and ultimate fate of Charny's *Questions* are almost entirely obscure. Intended for presentation to the Prince and the members of the Order of the Star they may have been, but we have no proof that this exercise actually took place.[45] If it did, and answers were offered to the various questions or even only some of them, those answers did not survive.[46] For modern readers of the document, an important question, perhaps more answerable than whether the questions were discussed in public, is, did King Jean and Geoffroi de Charny intend for discussion of Charny's list to prompt actual legislation by royal authority? Or perhaps, was the consideration of these questions simply meant as an educational exercise (as it clearly was in the case of such questions as W90 on *sens* v. *prouuesc*), to get the leading knights of France to think seriously about the standards by which they supposedly lived?

The second possibility may indeed appeal disproportionately to modern professors of medieval history, as both Dr. Boulton and I have given serious consideration to it in other books. This time around, I have come to the conclusion that the "educational exercise" possibility is unlikely. The evidence taken as a whole shows that King Jean was rather serious about restoring the old standards of chivalry that made France great in the past. His Order of the Star was one of his most important tools to do that, and from the beginning he visualized it as an advisory body. I simply find it too far-fetched to think that in the midst of various crises, King Jean would have wasted a rare opportunity to talk to and influence some of the most important warriors in his kingdom. If such discussion was going to take place among members of the order in his presence, then I believe the king would have expected definite results. It is interesting that such a discussion based on Charny's *Questions* would have included very little that touched upon royal authority and loyalty of the *chevalerie* of France to its monarch, but this is not an insuperable objection to the scenario I am sketching out. King Jean might have found it very useful to pose as the patron of the good old days and the good old ways, respecting and promoting aristocratic privilege and influence, and still have felt that he was gaining something from the exercise. If he thought of himself as an Arthur-like figure, he might sincerely have believed that he was upholding old, vital, standards. Likewise Charny: this is a man of very definite opinions, a man who could cajole his contemporaries with such phrases as "there are no small feat of arms, only good and great ones,"[47] but who did so specifically to urge them to heroic measures. He too, given the choice, would not waste his time with a mere theoretical exercise.

Thus I believe we can approach the *Questions* as a serious, practical prelude to legislate "on matters of arms," even if some questions might have been less relevant to that purpose. The project was abortive; no answers survive, and no legislation was issued by King Jean on the matters that were identified by his advisor as worthy of discussion and judgment.

It would be interesting indeed to know who, and how many read Charny's works. The answer seems to be that Charny was not read, or at least his works were not copied, after the fifteenth century. The editors of modern times identify nine manuscripts (one lost since the 18th century) which contain one or more Charny works. Editions have been scarce, too. I am aware of no edition before Kervyn de Lettenhove included the *Book of Chivalry* in his edition of Froissart's works. In the twenty-first century, only the *Book of Chivalry* is easily available. Yet if Charny knew the extent of his literary success, he might not be disappointed. Charny manuscripts are associated with two of the most important rulers of early fifteenth century France. The Brussels manuscript which is considered the best source of the text bears the arms of Jean the Fearless, Duke of Burgundy from 1404–19; this manuscript is also the best exemplar of the *Questions.* Another manuscript bearing signs of patronage of the high nobility is in Paris; its copy of *Charny's Book* bears the arms of the Duke of Bedford, the regent of France for the Lancastrian claimant Henry VI. If Charny had hoped for an influential readership, one could hardly hope for better than the two men who seem to have owned luxury copies of his work. A half-century after his death, Charny's ideas were still known and perhaps undergoing a revival, but succeeding generations forgot him.

His ultimate obscurity—at least until the current revival of interest—does little to reduce the usefulness of his writings for those who wish to explore the history of war and the influence of chivalry on warriors of the mid-fourteenth century. In particular, the almost entirely neglected *Questions* can be read as a reflection of the priorities and opinions of one of the most experienced and renowned warriors of his time.

Endnotes

1. This is Kennedy's phrase, which she inserts on p. 85 of her translation of the *Book of Chivalry* as a subtitle.
2. Something over a thousand lines of verse are devoted in *Charny's Book* to description of the dangers and challenges of the three types of deeds of arms, and a similar long section in the *Book of Chivalry* treats jousting, tourneying, and war in order.
3. Kaeuper and Kennedy, 87.
4. W58 and Rossbach, 153 n. for 65, 10.
5. Crouch's chapter "Reconstructing Chivalry," in *The Birth of Nobility: Constructing Aristocracy in England and France, 950–1300* (Longman, 2005), 7–28, is a valuable discussion.
6. Kaeuper and Kennedy, 158; Kennedy's insertion of the subtitle "the men-at-arms of supreme worth" at 155 has the potential to confuse re: Charny's terminology.
7. "Orde" is found at Kaeuper and Kennedy, 166.
8. See Boulton, 178, quoting the king's letter of election.
9. Kaeuper and Kennedy, 173.
10. Kaeuper and Kennedy, 175.
11. Michael Anthony Taylor, 19 (line 457).
12. Kaeuper and Kennedy, 183.
13. Kaeuper and Kennedy, 43.
14. Kaeuper and Kennedy, 87.
15. Kaeuper and Kennedy, 99.
16. Kaeuper and Kennedy, 113.
17. Kaeuper and Kennedy, 127
18. Kaeuper and Kennedy, 117.
19. Used in the wide sense; the Order of the Star is not mentioned.

20. (London: Routledge & Kegan Paul, 1965).
21. Keen, *Laws of War,* 15–6.
22. S.J. Allen and Emilie Amt (eds.), *The Crusades: A Reader* (Peterborough, Ont.: Broadview Press, 2003), 305.
23. Allen and Amt, 168. A later section attempted to regulate gambling by rank.
24. *Matthew Paris's English History,* tr. J. A. Giles (London: Bohn, 1854) 2:354-5.
25. The 15th-century ordinances of Henry V preserved in the *Black Book of the Admiralty,* ed. Sir Travers Twiss, 4 vols. (London: Longman & Co., 1871), 1:459–73, late as they are, may be more typical, though his, too, came down to us because of the prestige of Henry's victories, which were attributed in part to his harsh discipline. A recent re-examination by Anne Curry: "The military ordinances of Henry V: texts and contexts," in Chris Given-Wilson, Ann Kettle and Len Scales (eds.), *War, Government and Aristocracy in the British Isles, c.1150-1500: Essays in Honour of Michael Prestwich.* Woodbridge, UK, Boydell Press: 2008, 214–249.
26. It is worth noting that Henry V's Ordinance at Mantes, c.21, Twiss, 1:465 on keeping watch on the camp, relates to W32, one of Charny's rare questions on camp management. See also Richard II's ordinance at Durham (1385), translated in an appendix below.
27. Text in *Ordonnances des Roys de France de la troisième race,* ed. D.F. Secousse , IV (Paris, 1734), 67–70; tr. in large part in *Society at War: the experience of England and France during the Hundred Years War,* ed. C.T. Allmand (New York: Barnes & Noble, 1973), 45–8.
28. Ercole Ricotti, *Storia delle compagnie di ventura in Italia,* 4 volumes (Turin, 1847) 1:349–66, 2:293–440.
29. Philippe de Remi, Beaumanoir, and Amédée Salmon, *Coutumes de Beauvaisis; texte critique pub. avec une introduction, un glossaire et une table analytique* (Paris: A. Picard et fils, 1899).
30. *Tractatus de bello, de represalis et de duello,* ed. Thomas Erskine Holland (Oxford: Oxford U.P., 1917).
31. *L'Arbre des Batailles d'Honoré Bonet* [sic], ed. Ernest Nys (Brussels, 1883); I have cited from *The Tree of Battles of Honoré Bonet* [sic], tr. G.W. Coopland (Liverpool: Liverpool U.P., 1949).
32. Giovanni da Legnano, xiv-xvi.
33. *Tree of Battles,* 79–80.
34. *Tree of Battles,* 15.
35. *Tree of Battles,* 159 (4:56).
36. Bouvet makes one reference to the *Usaiges d'armes* (Giovanni da Legnano, 140; *Tree of Battles,* 153) in connection with a master setting a reasonable ransom on a prisoner, "according to the usage of arms and of his country." King Jean's ordinance (n. 68 above), which for all we know Charny had a hand in, says that those military leaders who break the ordinance will be punished "according to reason, custom and *les droit d'armes.*"
37. Wright, *Knights and Peasants: The Hundred Years War in the French Countryside* (Boydell Press, 1998), 42–3.
38. Wright, 423.
39. See his short description of the *Questions* on p. 43.
40. Wright, 10, 12 discusses why the word "soldier," which in the 14th century designated only salaried warriors and often dependent ones, is not a good general term in this period.
41. Keen, *Laws of War,* 19; at 1, Keen translates a passage from Froissart shows French knights using the phrase "law of arms" (Froissart 8:43) as a shibboleth demanding honorable treatment. Beaumanoir treats *guerre* as a privilege; see above at n. 70.
42. Kaeuper and Kennedy, 139–147.
43. Kaeuper and Kennedy, 178–9.
44. Note that tourneys seem to have become extinct in England and France in the 1340s. They continued for a few decades in the Low Countries, and there were later revivals in a number of other places. Crouch, *Tournament,* p. 130–1.

45. Simply reading through all the questions takes enough time that it seems unlikely in the extreme that a full debate on the law of arms could be finished in any one meeting of the order.
46. *Tirant lo Blanc,* the fifteenth-century chivalric novel, shows characters interested in debating the kind of issues treated by Charny. Joanot Martorell and Martí Joan de Galba, *Tirant lo Blanc,* tr. David H. Rosenthal (New York: Schocken Books, 1984).
47. Kaeuper and Kennedy, 87.

3 CHARNY'S JOUSTERS AND TOURNEYERS

It has been said before, but it bears repeating, that Charny's *Questions*, like his other two books, are not just about war, but also about chivalric sport; his subjects and his audience are not just warriors, but jousters and tourneyers. This interest, Charny's insistence on treating sport and *guerre* together as *armes*, gives his literary accomplishment a special character.

Charny's patron, Jean II, in his plans and arrangements for the Order of the Star was clearly motivated by the feeling that too many knights put too much value on friendly, even celebratory, exercises and displays of martial skill, when what France needed was for the military aristocracy to devote themselves to warfare. The Order of the Star was meant to revitalize chivalry in France, in part by giving its highest honors only to those who excelled in war, in part by charging the order's members to commit themselves to fighting to the finish, without thought of retreat or running away. Charny, too, preached in *Charny's Book* and the *Book of Chivalry* that fighting in war was the source of the greatest honor, and when done for just cause, the worthiest pursuit of a Christian man.

Yet Charny knew that a discussion of chivalry, or the *métier* of the warrior, or the acquisition of honor by men-at-arms, or the laws that governed their activities would be drastically incomplete if jousting and tournaments were ignored. Charny's writings all follow a common plan in which jousting, tournaments, and war were depicted as a sequence of honorable, more honorable, and most honorable activity. Charny certainly thought that warfare was the acme of the true warrior's career, but participation in the two lesser pursuits he never criticized. "There are no small feats of arms, only good and great ones," he stated in the *Book of Chivalry*.[1] Charny valued jousting and tournaments for their role in preparing warriors, especially the young, for more demanding challenges. He also recognized that his audience was heavily invested in these lesser martial activities, and shaped his rhetoric so as not to alienate those he wished to influence. Charny saw that jousts and tournaments were important to the social identity of the military aristocracy of his country; as we shall see, how one participated in jousting was one way a knight might show his rank and distinguish himself from mere squires, while the structure of tournaments emphasized distinctions between different kinds of knights and perhaps excluded squires. Anything that purported to be an in-depth discussion of the law of arms must treat jousts and tournaments as well.

Jousting

In my earlier book, *Jousts and Tournaments*,[2] I did my best to analyze the rules for chivalric sport as they are incompletely revealed by Charny's questions. I will not repeat that analysis here, especially since two important works have been published since. David Crouch's excellent book *Tournament*[3] has filled in our picture of tournaments, the tournament culture and the relationship between tourneys and jousts, especially for the twelfth and thirteenth centuries.

Noel Fallows' encyclopedic *Jousting in Medieval and Renaissance Iberia*[4] makes widely available a distinct and richly documented regional tradition. My discussion here will look at those jousting and tourney questions that shed a particular light on the values and attitudes of Charny's knightly audience.

We should begin with defining and distinguishing between the two most important chivalric sports.

Tournaments or tourneys seem to have originated in France in the late eleventh century, when armored cavalry was newly important in warfare. The tourney honed the skills necessary for effective group maneuvers. In early tournaments, as in the battles of the time, team members combined their efforts to capture knights and their mounts; the horses and the equipment were kept by the captors, and in the twelfth century, at least, the defeated knights were required to ransom themselves, much as in serious warfare.[5] Tournaments, therefore, can be best visualized as mock battles, which might involve striking opponents with weapons—Charny especially associated the tournament with the use of the edge of the sword[6]—or even wrestling them to the ground. The term *mêlée,* which originally meant "a mixture," came to be applied to the fighting in a cavalry battle or tournament and to mean "a confused struggle."

Jousts, too, were often competitions between teams, as we will see in a moment, but they were quite different from mêlées. In a jousting match, an individual from one team charged another and tried to knock his opponent off his horse with a lance. The opponent, of course, was doing the same.

Jousting as a sport likely grew out of individual confrontations that took place between armies or tournament teams before the groups themselves came into contact. Confrontations between champions representing rival armies have been part of many a warrior culture, and are well documented in Western Europe from the eleventh to the fourteenth centuries.[7] Preliminary fights in the form of jousts (*commençailles,* or in Charny's *Questions, encommensaille*) preceded the mêlées in the late twelfth-century French tournaments in which the famous William Marshal participated.[8] Jousts apart from tourneys were certainly a feature of chivalric life in the thirteenth century.[9] In Charny's time the joust was a favorite martial activity. Although professional soldiers may have sometimes scorned jousting as a presumptuous and foolish waste of time,[10] it appealed to many others. During the early phase of the Hundred Years War the seeking out of adventures or "deeds of arms" in a contested borderland (such as the Scottish march or the Anglo-French frontier near Calais) was a popular pastime. Such adventures usually involved jousting.[11] Jousts of peace were frequent, too, occasionally celebrating such important occasions as a royal marriage or a diplomatic event.

Jousting as discussed in the first section of the *Questions* and in the first few lines of the *Book of Chivalry,* is a deed of arms of peace. Although Charny does not say so, this means jousting with blunted lances, the kind which often takes place at "festivities," an attractive pursuit that is "fair to see."[12] (Unfortunately for us, Charny shows no interest in describing the colorful details that would help us visualize this fair spectacle.) There was another, more deadly, type of jousting, in which the competitors rode against each other using steel-pointed lances. These jousts were properly classified as *guerre,* and are treated briefly by Charny in his questions on the law of arms for war. Such jousts, the "adventures" or "deeds of arms" referred to above, were probably only thought appropriate for challenges between enemies, or subjects of different, hostile lords. We see an example in Charny's first question on war (W1). The question treats a dispute over the possession of a horse between two warriors in the same army, one who has lost the horse to an enemy champion in a morning joust, and the second who has taken the horse from its new owner in a joust that same evening.

If the jousts of Charny's first set of questions are less deadly than they might be, and are associated in Charny's mind with enjoyable festivities, nevertheless such "friendly" jousting was taken very seriously, and for good reason. Jousting even among friends was a dangerous and high-stakes game in which competitors often[13] risked the loss of their horses in hopes of winning their rivals' mounts. The possession of horses is the dominant issue in the questions on jousting. We see in J1, a case which seems to present basic characteristics of the jousting match, this formulation:

> *(J1) First I ask: An emprise for jousting is announced for a certain place on a certain day to deliver all knights of three lances and not more, and nothing else is announced except the prize. So it happens that one knight knocks another to the ground and out of the saddle with a stroke of the lance. Will he who knocks the other to the ground win the other's horse? What do you say in this case, will it not be judged by the law of arms?*

The joust is set up as a "typical" joust, with generic characteristics. Charny states these characteristics as generally as possible so he can focus his audience's attention on the main business: in normal circumstances, does a jouster who unseats his opponent gain his opponent's mount (a warhorse good enough to be used in a jousting competition)? That Charny repeatedly asks the same question about other cases indicates the answer to J1 must be yes. Warhorses were not cheap, and owning one or being able to borrow one from one's lord or an employer was a prerequisite to being considered a warrior of standing, or as contemporaries often put it, "a good man-at-arms."[14] The centrality of horses in the minds of jousters is illustrated by the fact that the majority of the *Questions on the Joust* can be summarized thus: "[Under certain circumstances] will he who knocked the other down win the horse?" Furthermore, almost all of the other jousting questions treat cases where a horse has been injured or killed, and the issue is whether one jouster owes another jouster compensation, as for example here:

> *(J7) Charny asks: An emprise is arranged for jousting by either knights or squires, with the announced rules as above. So it happens that one of the home team jousts in this way with one of the visitors, and because he was running out of bounds, the visitor throws his lance and the thrown lance strikes its butt end on the ground. And before the front end falls down it pierces the other's horse and kills it. Does the visitor give recompense for the horse? What do you say?*

Out of twenty questions, exactly one has nothing to do with the possession or the value of a horse:

> *(J16) Charny asks: A knight of the emprise described above strikes his spurs and in his first course is wounded and disarms himself; and another puts on his harness and mounts his horse to joust in the place of him who was wounded with the agreement of the wounded man, even though he was not at all part of the emprise, but is only to aid those who had established the emprise. So he jousts so well that none of the home team in the judgment of all comes even close to him. Who will have the prize, he who jousted so well, or his master for whom he jousted, or whoever has jousted best among those holding the emprise next to him? What do you say?*

Jousting question 16 directs our attention to a key term, *emprise,* which we must come to grips with if we are to understand the organization and even the psychology of jousting matches. *Emprise* is a common Middle French term which means "enterprise, undertaking," and a number of other things, such as initiative and audacity. As a military term it can mean an expedition or exploit or even an attack or an assault, with the implication that military initiative is being taken or skill is being applied.[15] In Charny's usage however *emprise* seems to have a more specialized meaning or set of related meanings.

If we return to J1 we see that the generic jousting match described there springs from an agreement among a group of knights to accomplish a specific deed of arms, "to deliver all knights of three lances and not more." In other words, these knights have committed themselves to meet any knight who wishes to come against them and run three lances or courses—and no more.[16] This agreement or commitment seems to be called "the *emprise*"; at the same time *emprise* appears also to mean the terms of the collective commitment (all knights; three lances; an unspecified prize) and even the group which has made the commitment. As we saw above, question J16 speaks of two different knights, one the master (presumably the captor) of the other. The master is "a knight of the *emprise*" the other is not; one is qualified to win an agreed-upon prize, the other may not.

The jousting questions show that whoever established an *emprise* had a certain amount of freedom to define the game; but Charny wanted to know in the case where the announcement of the *emprise* did not cover a contingency, or the jousting was so informal that there was no announcement, how an unanticipated problem was to be resolved. In delivering these questions to the Knights of the Order of the Star, Charny was placing the responsibility on warriors themselves to know and apply their own customs, which he called "the law of arms for jousting" (J 20). It seems very likely, however, that Charny had a limited faith that this would be a simple process. At some stage or another, principles and rulings were going to have to be argued and resolved.

Beyond arguments about the winning and losing of horses, Charny anticipated disagreements between the warriors about who was qualified to take part in various kinds of jousts. In the generic joust described in J1, the knights of the *emprise* are challenging other knights. This would seem to be the normal expectation, since eleven of twenty jousting questions specify "*emprises* for knights" or terminology to the same effect.[17] There were other kinds of jousting matches. One was the "*emprise* for squires." How different such an *emprise* was from a knight's *emprise,* and whether the law of arms required strictly separate competitions seems to have been a vexed question. Charny's J12 and J13 give us little to work with:

> *(J 12) A squire, completely armed for jousting, enters an emprise for knights and jousts; and a knight of the emprise knocks him out of the saddle with the stroke of the lance. Will the knight win the horse, for each believed that he was a knight until he was down, but he did not wear any golden accouterments. How will it be judged according to the law of arms?*
>
> *(J 13) A knight, armed as a knight, enters and jousts in an emprise for squires; and a squire in the emprise knocks him out of the saddle with a stroke of the lance. Will the squire win the horse? What do you say? What do others think?*

In the first question, there is a focus on the squire's equipment. He did not usurp the insignia of knighthood by wearing golden accouterments, and therefore presumably deserved no punishment on that account; people mistook him for a knight because he was "completely armed for jousting." We can surmise that he might have worn something different, perhaps lighter armor, if he was taking part in an *emprise* for squires.

If we look in the historical record for competitions for squires, or competitions where participants wore lighter armor, we can find both. In the twelfth and thirteenth centuries there were martial games called *behourds*. The participants wore light armor or sometimes none, and their weapons were restricted, in many cases to lance and shield. Some early *behourds* are stated to be competitions between squires. One fifteenth-century manuscript describes *behourds* as a form of joust between equal numbers, rather than a melee or tournament.[18] What little information we have, then, suggests that the *behourd* was a training exercise or a light-hearted —if still somewhat dangerous—recreation, one that could reasonably be done in lighter armor, and which perhaps was an early form of the joust. It might have been suitable for or restricted to squires. What little we can see of Charny's "*emprise* of squires" gives a quite similar impression. To speculate a bit further: there may have been less at stake in the squire's *emprise*. The same fifteenth-century manuscript that identifies *behourds* with jousting between equal numbers also states that the prize for the best behourder actually went to the heralds who organized the event, since they received no fees for supervising a *behourd*.[19] Could it be, then, a squire's *emprise* was a low-cost, low-risk event in which unhorsed jousters kept their horses? And, contrariwise, that the squire in J12 likely lost his horse, despite his lack of golden spurs, because that was normal in a knights' *emprise*?

On the other hand the point of questions J12 and J13 may be the conflict between perceptions of status based on observation, and formally assigned rank. Ideally, one should be able to look at the armed man in the lists and tell by the armor he wears whether he belongs in an *emprise* for knights or an *emprise* for squires. But in fact it is easy to make a mistake. It may be that there are scofflaws or showoffs taking the formalities lightly; such an attitude may account for the behavior of the squire in the armor good enough for a knight who enters a knights' *emprise*, or of the well-armored knight who insists on jousting against squires in a competition reserved for them and perhaps requiring the lighter armor worn by most squires, at least in the past. However pressing these problems may have been in the real world of 1352, Charny thought questions of status were important enough in the context of jousting, well on its way to becoming the premiere chivalric sport, to offer several questions which hung on the use and abuse of rank. Likewise, in the *Questions on War*, we find Charny turning quickly (W3, 4, 5) to the rules that govern *emprises* fought with steel lances. In this context, it also seems to matter whether a man-at-arms is a knight or a squire:

> *(W3) Knights joust with steel lances in an emprise... Will the one who has knocked the other to the ground out of the saddle win the horse?*
> *(W4) Do squires have the same rights as knights in such a case?*
> *(W5) [If] a knight knocks a squire out of the saddle with a steel lance, or a squire a knight, what right will he have to the horse, or will it neither be lost nor gained?*

When it comes to warlike activities which set man against man and which were freighted with considerations of personal honor, all men-at-arms are not equal—at least a thorough authority on the law of arms would want to discuss how knights and squires differed.[20] But in actual practice perhaps the differences were not great. After all, J6 shows "knights and squires joust[ing] in an *emprise*..." and J7 postulates "an *emprise*...arranged for jousting by either knights or squires." We know that it would be common at the end of the fourteenth century to admit squires to competitions where they faced knights on the basis of apparent equality, even on the most prestigious occasions. Richard II's internationally-advertised jousts at Smithfield in 1390 featured a day where the king's champions, all knights, ran courses against both knights and squires.[21] Earlier that same year at St. Inglevert, English squires as well as knights faced three French champions of high rank in a competition in which the honor of the rival kingdoms was at stake. No one remarked on their inclusion in such a high-profile event. Indeed, a grant of arms issued by Richard II in 1389 to one John Kingston confirms that at this time the rank of squire was a good and sufficient qualification to perform honorable deeds of arms with a foreign knight. John Kingston, a warrior of indeterminate status, had been challenged by a Frenchman, and so that he "should be more honorably received and be able to do and perform the said deeds and points of arms," King Richard "received him in the estate of gentleman and make esquire and wish that he should be known by the arms and henceforth carry these, namely, Argent, with a chapeau azure with an ostrich plume gules." John Kingston was elevated to undoubted gentility when he simultaneously acquired royally-sanctioned heraldry and the title or status of squire.[22]

If we can't be sure what degree of equality Charny's companions in the Order of the Star would have been willing to grant squires in the context of jousting, the repeated wrestling with the issue of participation by squires suggests that they could not be easily "kept in their place." No longer were they military servants far below the knights in status. Their growing importance in warfare was undoubtedly one cause of this development. Jean II's ordinance, concerned as it was in attracting well-armed French warriors into military service, pragmatically recognized that squires with coats of arms, men like John Kingston, were a military resource whose wages were worth specifying. At almost exactly the same time, according to an anonymous account of the famous Combat of Thirty against Thirty, Breton squires who bore coats of arms were considered as important in the defense of their province as the famous knights of the country.[23] As we shall see in our discussion of the questions on war, the difference in dignity between knight and squire in some contexts seemed not just less important than it used to be, but almost irrelevant. Thus the uncertainty that might surround the case described in J12.

Jousting was the least, by Charny's own reckoning, of the three types of military activity, yet it touched on vital issues of rank and identity. The intense interest in horses revealed in the first section of the *Questions* reveals how important possession of a good horse remained to the knight, especially the aspirant knight. That knights argued about the rules and the conduct of formal combats can scarcely be doubted; narrative sources from a variety of times and places, and particularly Charny's own fourteenth century show competitors intent on winning the most favorable judgment on their performance from their fellow warriors, and thus willing to argue about and manipulate the rules.[24] If Charny is to be believed, however, there was no better cause for an argument than the issue of who got the horse that gave *chevaliers* their name.

Tournaments

Jousting could be part of an elaborate occasion, but a match could be arranged by a fairly simple announcement, and it could be indulged in completely informally, with no announcement. Nevertheless we have seen that participation in even the friendliest joust was potentially a very serious matter. The tournaments treated by Charny in the second set of questions were, if anything, more serious yet. Although they may have been less bloody and destructive than campaigns in war, they required a tremendous outlay of physical assets and commitment of organizational resources, the same ones used in war itself. Even if we exclude consideration of personal danger—as Charny consistently does—we are struck by how much was at risk.

Charny's questions on tourneys pose a lot of difficult, indeed insoluble, puzzles. Neither Charny nor any other medieval writer before him felt it necessary to describe tournament rules and practice in a systematic manner. Much of our evidence comes from literary treatments that take it for granted that the audience knows a great deal about how tournaments were normally run, and use that shared knowledge as a background for the praise of a historic or legendary hero, or even a satire. Further, the bulk of this evidence is from well before the fourteenth century.[25]

There are two later treatises on the organization of tournaments texts that are of some use in reconstructing Charny's tourneys. The better-known one is by René, duke of Anjou and titular king of Sicily, who in the 1450s or '60s wrote a plan for a model tourney, *A Treatise on the Form and Organization of a Tournament.*[26] René's book prescribes exactly what should be done to stage an elegant festival and deed of arms. Yet it can only be used with the greatest caution. Not only did René write a full century after Charny, it was a century in which tourneying was almost extinct in France. We have no record that René ever took part in or sponsored one.[27] René may have been writing a work of creative anachronism, an homage to the practice and values of the good old days.[28] The second treatise, *The Old Manner and Regulation of the Tourney,*[29] also refers to some uncertain past. This was written by Jean Courtois, known as Sicily Herald, who despite his title was the product of a French environment, specifically the county of Hainaut in present-day Belgium. Sicily Herald died in 1437, and so his work is somewhat closer in time to the *Questions* than René's *Treatise.* Nevertheless, the gap is still large and we cannot tell what period of tournament practice, if any, Sicily Herald's description reflects. It provides us with some additional information about tournament organization, but like René's book, it cannot resolve our puzzles, only provide suggestions.

Tournaments, we know from a number of sources across various periods, involved hundreds, if not thousands, of participants, and many spectators and support personnel on top of that. They took place in large stretches of countryside between designated cities, while the cities themselves provided lodging for attendees. Tournaments thus took over whole regions and no doubt subjected them temporarily to "the law of arms for tourneys. (T1, T2)" Charny hints at the busy atmosphere of tournament time in a couple of places. In T1, Charny shows a "powerful man" (*uns riches homs*) forcing a banneret whom he has had under contract before to return to his service and makes him "display his arms outside the windows with him." What that means is both described and illustrated in René's book:

> *...immediately after a lord or baron arrives at the inn, he should display his coat of arms in the window...and the barons who put up their banners at the windows are required on their honor to display the coats of arms of at least five other tourneyers with their banners, as a company.*[30]

As usual, Charny brushes past the colorful custom to focus on a legal conflict. Similarly,

> *(T21) A knight and two squires are contracted for the tourney and for the year. The knight hastily comes into the city where he wishes to tourney, doesn't find his squires, and retains two others on the eve of the tourney. And when the morning comes the two squires who are retained for a year come before the hour of "tie it up!" and present themselves to him ready to serve him. The master refuses them for the day, for this day he has retained two others. Then the two squires retained for a year go to seek their gain with other masters for a year, and say they are able to do it. The first master says no. What will be judged in this case by the law of arms for tourneys?*

We are allowed to visualize the crowds and confusion that led to this problem, but for Charny it is just the background for a case of the "employment law" that applied to tournament participants.

It is important to remember that taking part in tournaments required either assembling a retinue, or hiring oneself out to the leader of a retinue, or both. A banneret by definition was a leader of a group of lesser knights, but he hired himself and his retinue to someone more powerful. A knight bachelor, even though he might well be an employee at the bottom of a hierarchy of knights, would be an employer of squires, as we have just seen. Thus one very important aspect of the tourney was the network of contracts that held tourneyers together into teams.

Or proved insufficient to do so. The employment law cases devised by Charny (T1–4, T20–21) suggest that the subordinate parties to contracts were keenly aware of the advantages and disadvantages of contractual arrangements and that they were willing to withdraw their services and go elsewhere if they were unhappy with their lord for not providing opportunities for profit. The dispute in T1 was initially triggered by the fact that a banneret (or knight) had ridden to a tourney with his own expensive retinue only to find his lord apparently unwilling to compete. The knight may have been faced with a direct loss if the lord was not paying tourney expenses on this occasion; more frustrating, perhaps, was the loss of hoped-for gain. The banneret may have felt that this loss of opportunity constituted breach of contract, and struck another, better and longer-term contract. A similar expectation by retainers is found in T20 and 21. In the first, "a banneret comes during the week to tourney and does not wish to take part at his rank, but to take part under another as a bachelor." Some "companions [knights] who are retained by him for a year" demand maintenance, but are refused; they then feel justified in seeking a contract with another lord. In T21 we have essentially the same situation one step farther down in tourneying society; the knight who could not find his squires hires others in their place. The loss of that day's tourneying and associated payments is enough of an affront to lead them to abandon their agreement with the knight and find another.

All of Charny's questions are fictions devised to illustrate a principle, but some of the cases must have seemed more likely than others. When it came to labor disputes it seemed worthwhile to debate whether contracted knights who were offered a better deal could take it. In T1 the powerful man whose retainer has left seems at first to be confident that he can force the retainer to come back and "display his arms outside the windows with him." But Charny found it interesting and useful to disappoint this invented figure and plunge him into a bidding war (T2). "So the powerful man who had retained that banneret for a season... has lost him for the year," and so he offers his former retainer a property or income for life. The new employer resists. But in T3 this second powerful man is put into the position of offering a hereditary benefit to avoid losing his new retainer. We have no idea how common such bidding wars were, but the possibility of such things inspired a certain amount of anxiety among the Knights of the Star.

As in the case of the joust, the single most important issue in the tournament was the possession of horses. Some readers may know that in the days of William Marshal, warriors, their horses, and their harness (personal and equestrian) had all been at risk. Charny, however, describes the action at a tourney as "losing and gaining horses" (T7).[31] When, in T9, some knights pull another to the ground, along with his mount, they "cut his girths and the breastplate of the saddle ...lead [the horse] to the stake and the knight remains on the ground with his saddle between his legs." If the competitors' freedom was not at risk, they were liable to be struck with weapons (T8, 18) or pulled to the ground (T6, 10, 18). When dozens or even hundreds were struggling for the control of valuable horses, the level of violence must have been impressive, as hinted at here:

> *(T18) Which is to be more highly prized: The one who loses two horses or three in one day while attacking or defending quite openly, or one who keeps his horse very close the whole day and endures and bears well the pulls and blows and everything that comes his way? What do you say?*

Yet however enthusiastically the riders may have thrown themselves into such competition, there was also a desire and need to limit the violence. One way this was done was through the provision of judges or *disceur*[32] who enforced a number of important rules. Such figures are known from a multitude of sources before and after Charny's time, and may have been heralds or respected warriors.[33] In the tournament questions we see *disceurs* fulfilling these functions: "[taking] the oath of the knights in the accustomed manner" (T5, 6); having "tie it up" (*le lacier*) cried as a warning to tourneyers to lace up their armor (T6, 7, 13); having stakes put in the field, to which captured opponent were to be taken during the tournament (T6, 7). The judges also had the responsibility to divide the competitors into two reasonably equal sides (T6, 7), to release them (to allow them to start the combat)(T6), and, presumably, at the end of the day to pull up the stakes and end the tourney (T11).

Clearly, the authority of the *disceurs* was considerable under "the law of arms for tourneys." Yet what Charny says about their duties is restricted in a familiar way. Take for instance the matter of the "accustomed" oath that the judges administered in T5. What was in that oath? Certainly important matters, since a bachelor who refuses to swear is prevented from taking part. René's treatise provides a text:

> *High and powerful princes, lords, barons, knights and squires, each and every one of you, please raise your right hand on high, towards the saints, and all together, as you will in the future, promise and swear by the faith and promise of your body, and on your honor, that you will strike none of your company at this tourney knowingly with the point of your sword, or below the belt, and that no one will attack or draw on anyone unless it is permitted, and also that if by chance someone's helm falls off, no one will touch him until he has put it back on, and you agree that if you knowingly do otherwise you will lose your arms and horses, and be banished from the tourney; also to observe the orders of the judges in everything and everywhere as they order delinquents to be punished without argument; and also you swear and promise this by the faith and promise of your body and on your honor.*[34]

Sicily Herald's treatise similarly shows (in his spelling) *diseurs* swearing competitors to use specific kinds of weapons and to refrain from interfering with any arrangements made by the *diseurs.*[35] Charny's questions on the tourney touch on none of the seemingly serious offenses or how such offenses might be punished. Typically, he wishes the case of the non-swearing bachelor to be examined because, after the tournament is finished, "those whose horses are lost ask for them back and say it was not a tourney at all." Once again, it is a matter of "who gets the horse?"

That all-important question evidently was capable of inspiring the most ingenious rules lawyering. Some of the most difficult questions in the entire collection circle around the idea that only in a "real" tourney is it legitimate to "gain and lose horses." Charny devotes three questions to asking his audience to define tourneying, *encommensailles,* and *toupineurs,* no doubt because the differences between them were unclear. If something which was advertised as a tourney was actually more like an *encommensaille,* perhaps the status of horse captures might be in doubt. The key issue seems to have been inclusivity. Tourney questions 6, 7, 13 and 14, taken as a group suggest that the results of a tournament might be challenged if every available knight did not participate. That presumably was why in T6 the losers felt they could ask for their horses back.

The incomplete T7 also shows a situation where some would-be tourneyers can't be allocated to a team because the combat has started too soon. There would seem to be room to complain that "this was not a tourney at all." Two more cases, T13 and T14, extend the possible grounds for challenge. It appears that some might claim that in a proper tourney all knights in a given city and surrounding area might be expected to take part, perhaps even be obligated to do so, even though they had shown no wish or readiness to compete:

> *(T 13) A tourney is arranged with mutually agreed rules in a city and the stakes are placed and "tie it up" is cried and they sally forth. And at the point where they are outside, one or two bachelors arrive in the city who are not able to have their horses or harness that day. And because of this they do not remain, nor do they join a troop nor attack. Will this be a tournament or not? What will you say in this case by the laws of arms for tourneys?*
> *(T 14) If they are between two cities and it happens just as it is described above, will these be tourneying or held to take part in preliminary fights (encommensaille)?*

Could a tournament indeed be retrospectively canceled or delegitimized because it was not inclusive enough? If this was done, was the tourney reclassified as some other type of competition, perhaps one in which horses were not at risk? But Charny himself appears to exclude that interpretation in T19: The knights bachelor in that case lost their horses in *encommensaille* and are petitioning their lord to buy them back. If horses were normally at risk in *encommensaille,* it is difficult to see what practical difference it would make whether the contest in T14 is called *encommensaille* or tourney.

Tourney questions 6, 7, 13, and 14 show that inclusiveness was a recognized characteristic of a "real tournament." In perhaps three and likely all four questions, some dissatisfied tourneyers are seeking a considerable concrete benefit, the return of lost horses, and driving the argument of inclusiveness as far as it can go, if not farther. Yet they ought to have had a real foundation on which to build their complaints, even if their fellows might ultimately reject their position. I have suggested elsewhere this rather speculative reconstruction: When warriors met at a tourney ground, some at least of the knights and great lords and retinues would save themselves, their best horses, and their best efforts for the main event, when, ideally, everyone present would take part. Considerations of both status and practicality would be operating here. Men of established reputation might not want to risk it in any other forum than the best available, a "real tourney." Victory in a tourney depended on the disciplined use of well-trained retinues, and it was only in the main tourney that entire retinues were committed, and that customary friends and allies would all bring their weight to bear. The lord who found that he had spent his efforts and squandered his equine capital in a contest where expected participants had been excluded for no very clear reason might indeed be very angry. If only one of these inclusivity questions is at all straightforward—T7, where willing tourneyers are excluded, perhaps through no fault of their own—we have to remember

Charny's purpose and method: principles can be illuminated not only by "realistic" statements of problems but also by extreme ones.

We should not leave the questions on tournaments without looking at a final issue, once again a familiar one: the participation of squires. Squires were certainly participants in tournaments long before Charny's time, but often in a subordinate capacity. The various ranks of knights who were the main players in the tourney were supplemented by servants both mounted and on foot. Fifteenth-century writers thought that men of rank were entitled to them, but also believed that the number should be regulated. Neither in the fourteenth nor fifteenth century were squires in the position of *varlez* (as René designated on-the-field servants), but earlier in Edward I of England's legislation of 1292, the participation of armed squires in a tourney was a privilege granted to their lords. Only a *gran siegneur* was allowed to be attended by armed squires, three of them, who could take part in the action and pull other tourneyers from their horses.[36]

Those three armed squires show up in Charny's questions:

> *(T10) A squire or two or three armed for the tourney find a knight outside of the mêlée. So they stop him and pull him down and take the horse off to the stake. When evening comes the knight demands his horse because there was no knight present at his loss. The squires say no. What should happen according to the law of arms for tourneys?*

Once again, we have to wonder, given the much greater agency and responsibility accorded to squires in practical warfare in the 1350s, whether this knight's insistence on rank's privileges on the tourney field really makes sense. Yet we have seen in regards to jousting that awareness of rank in such formal combats was a conceivable stance.

There is also a further possibility; we can ask, as David Crouch does, whether tourneying in the style depicted by Charny and earlier writers even existed when the questions were composed. Yes, it was still possible recall that a decade earlier Edward III had sponsored a tournament attracting a reported 250 knights.[37] Crouch, however, rates this as a rather small tournament by the standards of an earlier era, and it may have been one of the very last to take place in the Anglo-French aristocratic sphere. It may be that the respect shown the tourney in the *Questions* and Charny's other writings reflect a conservative streak in the mentality of Sir Geoffroi and his audience. The practices and rules that we see or sometimes infer from Charny's case studies may have been more than a bit old-fashioned.

Endnotes

1. Kaeuper and Kennedy, 87.
2. (Highland Park, TX: Chivalry Bookshelf, 2010).
3. (London: Hambledon and London, 2005).
4. (Woodbridge: Boydell Press, 2010).
5. Richard Barber and Juliet R.V. Barker, *Tournaments: Jousts, Chivalry and Pageants in the Middle Ages* (Woodbridge: Boydell Press, 1989), 1–27; Barker, *The Tournament in England 1100-1400* (Woodbridge: Boydell Press, 1986), 141–5.
6. Kaeuper and Kennedy, 88–9.
7. Matthew Strickland, "Provoking or Avoiding Battle? Challenge, duel, and single combat in warfare of the High Middle Ages," in *Armies, Chivalry and Warfare in Medieval Britain and France,* ed. Matthew Strickland (Stamford, Lincolnshire: Paul Watkins Publishing, 1998), 335–43.
8. Strickland, 335–7.

9. Barker, 88–89.
10. Jean le Bel, in his *Chronique,* 2:195, shows the English commander Brandebourch dismissing a suggestion for a joust between his champions and some Bretons because "this kind of venture was over too soon, and in it one got more of a reputation for presumption and folly than for honor and worth" (*car c'est une aventure de fortune trop tost passée, si en acquiert on plus le nom d'oultrage et de folie que d'onneur et de pris*).
11. Barker, 152–4.
12. Kaeuper and Kennedy, 87.
13. About four decades after Charny wrote, the Monk of St. Denis, in celebrating the spectacular joust at St. Inglevert, notes that the three French champions "returned the arms and horses which they were entitled to on account of their victories." *Chronique du Religieux de Saint-Denys,* ed. M. Bellaguet. 6 vols. (Paris, 1832–52) 1:682.
14. W54—a gentleman without a horse can only find employment as a foot sergeant.
15. For instance, in describing a failed expedition promoted and organized by the Haze of Flanders, Froissart uses the terms *exploit d'armes* (10:107) and *une folle emprise* (110).
16. The group of knights (the home team) are promising to deliver any visitors of their own oaths or self-imposed commitment to run three lances with some member of the home team. For more on oaths in connection with formal combats see *Deeds of Arms,* 67–8.
17. J1, 2, 3, (8), 11, 12, 14, 15, 16, 18, 20; J9 and 10 refer to a preceding "*emprise* as above," probably a reference to what appears to be an *emprise* for knights in J8.
18. Crouch, 113–5; Barker, 148 (squires), 149 (jousting between equal numbers, lance and shield only). Barber and Barker, 30, 153 (behourd at Windsor in *cuir boulli*), 164 (a 13th c. German behourd would have been a tourney if they had worn armor); 165 (Italian behourds played with no armor, only lance and shield).
19. Barker, 149.
20. See Froissart 9:490–2 and *Deeds of Arms,* 1–2 for a late 14th c. incident where an English squire was knighted so that he could fittingly meet a French champion.
21. According to the cryee; Froissart describes three days of jousting, knights vs. knights, squires vs. squires, and "knights and squires indiscriminately."
22. T. Rymer, *Foedera, Conventiones, Litterae, etc.* ed. G. Holmes, 20 vols. (London, 1704–35), 7:630.
23. H.R. Brush, ed., "La Bataille de trente Anglois et de trente Bretons," *Modern Philology* 10 (1912–3) : 87, 100–1.
24. E.g. Froissart, 12: 116–24; Muhlberger, *Jousts and Tournaments,* 88–90.
25. Crouch, *Tournament,* esp. 12–6.
26. Cited from *King René's Tournament Book: René d'Anjou, Traictié de la forme et devis d'ung tournoy,* tr. Elizabeth Bennett (n.p. 1992). http://www.princeton.edu/~ezb/rene/renehome.html, accessed January 10, 2014.
27. Barber and Barker summarize René's active career as participant and patron in *pas d'armes,* 114–7.
28. It must be said that in his heyday tourneys seem to have been making a comeback in both Flanders and Germany. Évelyne Van den Neste's chronology (*Tournois, joutes, pas d'armes dans les villes de Flandre a la fin du Moyen Age* (Paris: École des Chartes, 1996) 311–3, 318, 320) lists six Flemish tournaments in the 1450s, the decade in which René wrote. René, p. 1, says he used Flemish precedents. René also admitted to following the practices of Germany and Brabant.
29. In Ferdinand Roland, ed., *Parties inédites de l'œuvre de Sicilie, heraut d'Alphonse V roi d'Aragon, maréschal d'armes du pays de Hainaut, auteur du Blason des couleurs.* Publications de la Société des Bibliophiles des Belges séant à Mons, vol. 22 (Mons, 1867).
30. *King René's Tournament Book,* 10.
31. Sicily Herald's treatise uses similar phraseology twice in Roland, p. 182. The tournament ends with kings of arms pulling up the stakes and telling the knights "*vous ne poez huy perdre ne gaignier cheval.*" The treatise says disputes over *chevaux gaigniés ou perdus* are to be settled the day after the tournament by *droit d'armes.*

32. Crouch, *Tournament,* 89 translates this as "adjudicators."
33. Crouch, *Tournament,* 63–5, 89–90. In René's treatise, they are two knights and two squires chosen by the patrons and captains. *Joustes de Saint-Inglebert, 1389–90. Poème contemporaine,* ed. J. Pichon in *Partie inedited des Chronique de Saint-Denis* (Paris, 1864) 76-7, names one English and one French judge, who are not mentioned at all in the rest of the poem or in other accounts.
34. René, 15.
35. Roland, 180. What precisely the oath meant is unclear: "...prendoient la foi desditz chevalliers qu'ilz ne porteroient espées, armeurs, ne bastons affaittiés, n'efforceroeint les harnois ou estaches assises par les diseurs, et tendroient à bon le dit des diseurs." It may be that the competitors were swearing not to use "modified" equipment or gear fully "prepared" for war.
36. Barker, 57–9, 191–2.
37. This event at Dunstable is recorded by Adam Murimuth, *Continuatio Chronicarum,* in *Rerum Britannicarum Medii Aevi Scriptores (Rolls Series),* 93:123–4 and by Geoffrey le Baker, *Chronicon Galfridi le Baker de Swynebroke,* ed. Edward Maunde Thompson (Oxford: Clarendon Press, 1889), 75. Adam Murimuth's version notes that it took so long to get this huge event started "that nightfall prevented the affair from proceeding, so that scarcely ten horses were lost or gained."

4 CHARNY'S MEN-AT-ARMS

Men-at-Arms and Companions

A key phrase in Charny's *Questions on War* is the designation "men-at-arms." I shall begin analysis of the *Questions* by looking at how that phrase is used. We will particularly be interested in the contrast between the terminology Charny habitually uses to describe warriors and official French terminology of the same period.

Our guide to the official terminology is the ordinance we have seen before: the *Reglement pour le gens de Guerre*[1] of April 1351. This ordinance was aimed at advancing practical measures, financial and organizational, to attract well-armed warriors into military service through a raise in pay. It likewise defined procedures to make sure that those receiving pay were properly equipped.[2] The *Reglement* divides the army King Jean hoped to recruit into two unequal parts, mounted men and foot men. Each of these parts was further subdivided, as in this chart:

The Ideal Army of King Jean II of France April 30, 1351[3]

Mounted troops (Gens d'armes; Gens d'armes et Haubergeons)

Rank	Daily wage (sols tournois)
Banneret	40
Chevalier	20
Escuyer en costé de ses armes	10
Vallet... armé de habergeon...	5

Foot soldiers (Gens d'armes de pié; Pietons)

Type	Daily wage (sols tournois)
Arbelestier (crossbowman)	3
Pavesier (shieldman)	2½

At places in the *Reglement* there is a clear-cut contrast between *gens d'armes* and *gens de pié*, terms that identify cavalry and infantry. This by itself would lead us to conclude that all cavalry are *gens d'armes* and all *gens d' armes* are cavalry; the second seems to be true, but not the first. The document also categorizes mounted men using the phrase *gens d'armes et habergeons. Armes*, which can mean many things, here has the connotation of armor, good armor, or full armor. *Gens d'armes*, which can mean "warriors" or "fighting men" also in the context of this document means "fully armed and mounted men who are also bannerets, chevaliers, or 'squires with their own coat of arms'"—in other words, "warriors of noble or gentle status." Grouped with these undoubted *gens d'armes* are *gens de haubergeons*, mounted servants who accompany a man of higher status, and who are armored, but with mail shirts instead of more robust equipment available by 1351. We will have more to say about these "mail shirts" (i.e., the men who wore mail shirts) a bit later.

In the attempt of the *Reglement* to categorize "men-at-arms" we see an interesting struggle to make sense of traditional terms of status and equate them with categories at least partly defined by the equipment men bring with them. The king was very interested in that equipment, which implied that the man wearing it knew what to do with it. A knight banneret and the marginal figure known as a valet (an armed military servant, often quite young, dependent on a knight or squire)[4] were scarcely of equal importance or military value, but they were analogous in important ways, particularly in the fact that they brought vital equipment to the army, without which they and the army both would be ineffective. Similarly, all of these men-at-arms and "mail shirts" were mounted warriors. Military documents from a number of places in Europe show that in the fourteenth century archers and disciplined infantry grew in numbers and effectiveness, a phenomenon seen by some to be an important part of a "military revolution."[5] Yet those who paid for armies were still very concerned to have sufficient and well-mounted cavalry. Large amounts of money were spent to make sure that those who came to the army with good mounts got replacements of good quality if their horses were lost or killed. Much of the military bureaucracy was devoted to making sure that this vital function of replacing warhorses took place systematically, and without unreasonable expense or fraud. (This was as much the case in English armies as it was in French.)[6] Despite the arguments of a number of recent scholars that cavalry's importance in medieval warfare has been exaggerated, we can never forget the horses when thinking about the organization and workings of mid-fourteenth century armies.[7] Certainly Charny never did.

Little is said in this document about the men on foot; seven articles of the ordinance discuss men-at-arms and how they are to be organized, inspected, and deployed by the king's officers. Article 8 more or less says "we will do something similar in respect to foot men." (This clause does include information about what kind of protection crossbowmen and pavesiers, who carried large shields to protect their comrades from enemy archery, needed to be considered effective and worth paying for.)

If we turn to Charny's *Questions on War*, we find that his generic term for the men who fight is "men-at-arms." This is not to say that Charny is indifferent to such traditional designations as "knight," and "squire," among the "men-at-arms." Yet in both his *Book of Chivalry* and the *Questions on War*, Charny emphasizes similarities among respectable warriors, rather than emphasizing divisions of rank, saying in the former work that "many fine men-at-arms are as good as knights."[8] Perhaps in its original context this was a moral judgment, but it was also a practical one based on experience of war. In many respects knights and other men-at-arms did the same kind of work[9] and used similar equipment and tactics. However, "sergeants" or "valets," though mentioned, are held in little regard, as we shall see.

In the context of discussing the law of arms, "men-at-arms" had additional significance. The law of arms applied mainly to men-at-arms, to the point that the large number of archers, shieldmen, and unarmed servants accompanying fourteenth-century armies do not appear in the questions, though they surely featured in many a real-life legal dispute.[10] Further, men-at-arms are clearly those who define and perhaps even enforce the law of arms. The typical question in the *Questions on War* ends thus: "how shall [a given dispute between or affecting men-at-arms] be judged by the law of arms?" In several, however, the phrase is instead "what will be said about it by men-at-arms?" or something similar.[11] War Question 57 unambiguously ends with: "how should the men-at-arms judge the case?" In fact, except in one doubtful query which is only found in one manuscript,[12] there's hardly even a hint of any other judicial authority. Maurice Keen's discussion of the law of arms and its enforcement argued that military courts derived their authority from kings and their military deputies. Warriors of rank, commanders or royal lieutenants, were the judges, sometimes being advised by "*chivalers et esquires de valu.*"[13] In both the fourteenth and fifteenth centuries, ranking heralds decided some cases, while such non-military tribunals as the Parlement of Paris exercised special or appellate jurisdiction in regard to military matters.[14] But as far as Charny is concerned, disputes between men-at-arms—which constitute the bulk of the *Questions on War*—are settled by argument among men-at-arms. Thus in W10 a captain, sued for the replacement of their horses by men-at-arms who were under his command and under contract to him, seems to be in the position of arguing his case like anyone else; and a similar situation is found in W38.[15]

The rough equality of all men-at-arms at least in some circumstances is confirmed in a number of places. An equivalence is drawn between the term "men-at-arms" on one hand and the imprecise but not insignificant term "companion" [*compaings*] on the other. "Companion" does not simply mean the man who actually breaks bread with you in camp every morning; in fourteenth-century usage it can mean that, but it also means people of a certain military way of life, and a certain standing, who despite the fact they may oppose each other at times, share much. An excellent example can be seen in Froissart, where he writes about the great festive joust at St. Inglevert, which set former enemies, French and English and their allies, against each other in a time of truce. Froissart is intent on showing the event as a friendly occasion and so he is careful to put the friendliest face on all aspects of the competition. He portrays English knights and squires as reacting enthusiastically to the initial announcement by three French knights of an international joust. He shows them saying:

> *Let us prepare ourselves to go to this place near Calais: for these French knights only hold [the joust] that they may have our company: it is well done, and shows that they are good companions. Let us not disappoint them!*[16]

Likewise, question W1 shows two men from enemy armies jousting during a siege. They are called both "men-at-arms" and "companions." They are companions even though there is no apparent friendship between them; they use sharp spears against each other and each is intent on taking the horse away from the other. Similarly, leaders of the kind called "captains" in some questions are in W12 called "two companions… [who] are at war with each other"; they lead other companions, their friends, and their friends' followers into war. Thus leaders and followers share the identity of "companions." In another case, Charny casually and therefore significantly identifies his audience as companions: In W22, a "companion" is identified with a listening member of Charny's audience, "you."[17]

In some of the questions it seems that all men-at-arms were either knights or squires.[18] However, in others it is clear that in Charny's environment the social hierarchy was confused by the existence of sufficiently armored and mounted cavalrymen whose claims to gentility—family respectability—were weak or nonexistent. There was a stratum composed of non-squires and non-knights who could pass as men-at-arms who should, by the strictest standards, not have been allowed to do so. We meet such a figure in W69: a "knight or squire" only surrenders to one of his enemies after he is assured that the captor is a gentleman [*gentilz homs*] (a rare use of the term in the war questions).[19] The captive says "I surrender to you if you are a gentleman"; the other responds "I take you as a gentleman." When the captive "knight or squire" comes to the enemy city he soon figures out that the captor is "nothing but a sergeant [*sergens*][20] and no gentleman," and objects to members of the enemy garrison, who presumably *are* gentlemen, that his captivity is invalid. It is clear that Charny expects that he will win his case, since the next question begins:

> *If it was said that the knight or squire should not remain prisoner of the sergeant, will he go free or will he remain prisoner, and whose? (W70)*

We have here an interesting situation in which a mounted warrior is illegitimately exercising rights—specifically, the right to take gentle captives—that he is not entitled to. To the knowledgeable eye he almost, but not quite, passes for one of his betters; at the least he possesses a horse and some kind of armor. Was he a "mail shirt"? In danger of his life, "the knight or squire" has little choice but to surrender, but he has the presence of mind to register his doubt in the verbal contract he makes with his captor, who accepts his restriction. What is significant for our purposes, however, is that the captor sergeant dared to present himself as a full-fledged man-at-arms and was able to get away with it for a short time. This theoretical situation presented by Charny shows that the bottom edge of the category "men-at-arms" was a shadowy border zone.[21]

In W54 we get a hint that it may have been the horse ridden by the sergeant that allowed him to play his tricks on the battlefield. Here a gentleman without a horse takes employment as a "foot sergeant" [*sergens a pié*]. This means, according Charny, that he is not entitled to a share of the men-at-arms' booty, but only a share of the pooled booty allotted to the footmen—presumably meaning he will get less than any man-at-arms. But when it comes to time for action, the gentleman finds a horse and "is mounted on that day with the others who are well armed [*bien armez*]." A dispute results when the men-at-arms refuse to give the newly-mounted man a share of their booty. The main point of interest for us here is that having a horse—or perhaps having a good horse—is equivalent to being "well armed." We see again that at the bottom of the category man-at-arms, there is room for quite a bit of doubt about who belongs to it, and who benefits from the tangible and intangible benefits of being such a man. We are left confused; but the question makes no sense unless there was also room for confusion in 1352.

We can conclude this section by noting that having a good horse and demonstrating appropriate horsemanship was, in warfare as it was in jousting and tourneys, a key indicator of prestige and status. See W55: when a captain orders his men-at-arms to dismount and fight on foot, "many remain on horseback." Those who have obeyed the captain win the day; then those who stayed on horseback try to claim part of the booty, because all of them[22] were promised equal shares before the battle took place. It is hard to say whether the ones who remained mounted would overcome the objections of the (temporary) footmen about sharing in the booty. What is the chief interest at the moment is the little rebellion against taking a step down in the world, even when it was temporary and seemed to offer tactical advantage.[23]

Squires

Charny's *Questions on War,* like his *Questions on the Joust,* hints at some of the ambiguity that remained in the relations between knights and squires, and between them and the wider status of "man-at-arms."

Charny's usage of the word "squire" is not completely consistent, but is related to questions of social standing. It chiefly pops up in the *Questions on War* when they concern certain honorable activities that are certainly appropriate to knights. Charny is interested in presenting situations of this sort and asking whether squires can legitimately take part too. Once again, when it comes to warlike activities which set man against man and which are freighted with considerations of personal honor, all men-at-arms are not equal—though how great a difference there was in the treatment of men of different rank is quite unclear.

Four later questions in the War section indicate, however, that other personal confrontations between enemies may have been strongly affected by considerations of rank, which in a crisis may well have seemed more important than any brotherhood of men-at-arms. Two questions we have considered before: W69 and W70, which concern the "knight or squire" who is fraudulently captured by a sergeant pretending to be a gentleman. The implied answer to W69 is that this was indeed a fraud, and one more indication of the considerable status attained by squires by 1352; they were certainly gentlemen who were not to be abused by mere sergeants. Finally we have two similar questions, W21 and W65. In the first, one knight or squire strikes another and the second retaliates by taking him captive and shutting him up in a prison, and demanding a great ransom. Charny asks the question to find out whether taking prisoners for ransom is legitimate in peacetime, but we may also note that Charny stresses formal rank and does not designate the protagonists merely as men-at-arms. In W65, we see another knight or squire angrily reacting to the defiance of another, seemingly breaking the rules surrounding defiance by seizing his enemy immediately and not waiting for the next day as was usual.

Evidently there was a subtle calculus surrounding issues of honor, both in jousts in peacetime as part of celebrations, and confrontations that grew out of hostile warfare. Unfortunately we cannot reconstruct what the calculus was. It is truly unfortunate that we cannot discern what Charny himself thought about these issues.

The Near-Invisible Mass

King Jean's ordinance of 1352 gives us a fairly clear description of the personnel who made up his army. Charny, as one of the leaders of that military establishment, would have been keenly aware of the various types of warriors desired for the royal army and their roles in it. Thus it is particularly interesting that most of the personnel of a mid-fourteenth-century French army hardly appear in the *Questions.* All the attention is directed at the men-at-arms, who were less than half of any actual or planned French army.

Exact numbers of military men are difficult to ascertain in any historical era, but we can use figures compiled by Contamine with reasonable confidence. In his book, *Guerre, état et société à la fin du Moyen Age,* Contamine used a variety of sources, including financial records and proposals for campaigns that never took place to estimate French personnel in the years between 1337 and 1360.[24] We can see from these numbers the proportions of different kinds of troops were included or expected in early fourteenth-century armies. The official documents often divide the total personnel between men-at-arms, who in theory were all gentlemen, and the rest who would be common soldiers. When an army or a planned force was divided into more categories, one of those categories was always men-at-arms, and all the other categories would represent common soldiers of one sort or another.

Contamine's source material shows that with few exceptions, military planners in King Philip's and King Jean's France believed that an army should be or could be comprised of half mounted gentlemen (at most) and half (at least) of other troops, often on foot, who did not qualify as men-at-arms. In the earlier armies of King Philip VI's reign, the proportion of men-at-arms to other warriors was sometimes one in five (as in the case of the Gascon forces in 1339). As war progressed into the 1340s and 50s, armies for which we have planning documents or those actually assembled came closer, at least in their financial records, to the half-and-half arrangement. For example, the estates of Languedoc proposed in September and October 1356 to support an army of 5000 men-at-arms, 1000 sergeants, 2000 arbalestriers, and 2000 pavesiers. Even though the three latter groups were to be on horseback they were all common soldiers by contemporary standards.[25]

The French records use two general and three specific terms to identify types of combatants expected or desired by those assembling or financing armies. The general terms are *hommes* and *sergents,* both words which could mean retainer or servant and were used in a variety of contexts in both military and civilian life. Four specific terms refer to equipment or weapons used by specialized auxiliaries: archers, *arbalestriers* (crossbowman) and *pavesiers* (who lugged around large shields to protect against artillery fire). The use of these three terms suggests that the *hommes* and *sergents* did not use projectiles, but spears, lances, pikes or swords. All the preceding terms are qualified by one of the two phrases *de pie(d)* and *de cheval.* At the beginning of the Hundred Years War commoners were designated as foot troops, but as the second third of the century came to an end, a desire for more mobility led the French government to raise *sergents* or *arbalestriers* or other specialty troops *de cheval.* It should be made clear that their use of horses did not make *sergents* and such *hommes d'armes*—horses of indifferent quality were used for simple transport by all sorts of people—but one can understand that there might be room for confusion, as in the case of the mounted *sergent* who illegitimately claimed to be a gentleman (W69 and W70).

Despite the widespread use of the term *sergent,* and the omnipresence of the type the name represented, the fraudulent gentleman is one of only two *sergents* in Charny's *Questions on War.* The man who by nature is a commoner but pretends otherwise is matched by the gentleman by nature who for lack of a suitable horse has to take a contract as a *sergent a pie.* It seems individual *sergents* only crossed Charny's mind when they called into question considerations of status that were usually uncontroversial.

As for the *hommes de pie* of Contamine's documents, they have even more ghostly presence in the *Questions on War.* No individuals are identified whatsoever. As in the impersonal financial and organizational documents of the French crown, Charny uses *gens de pie* simply as placeholders or props. In W27, a great lord avoids battle even though he has a strong and capable army, "he has enough men-at-arms and foot to fight." In W32, a marshal assigns both horsemen and footmen to guard the camp, *le mareschal vont asseoir le gart de cheval et de pie.* At least *hommes* have this much of a role in Charny's army. *Arbalestriers, archers,* and *pavesiers* have none.

There is one more set of men who were always present in actual armies of the Hundred Years War who, since they had no independent role in the law of arms, are nearly invisible in Charny's questions. These are the servants who closely accompanied the men-at-arms. They were so vital to the performance of a man-at-arms that one must always presume that they are present even when they are not counted or specifically named: 1000 men-at-arms were always accompanied by 1000 servants on horseback. Most of these servants were perhaps scarcely armed and had only the smallest weapons. Some were very young and had been forced into service. They were not tied to the king's service or paid by royal officials, but directly by their master. The most common name for them was *valet*, though they were also known as *pillars*. *Pillars* was closely related to the word and idea of pillage, as the similar *brigan* (another term for non-noble warrior) gave rise to the word brigandage. Nicholas Wright has argued that pillage and brigandage were typical of the dirty work these servants performed—they were robbers on behalf of their gentleman masters, often the brutal face of war to the civilian population.[26] Charny knew these men: in the *Book of Chivalry* he said "there are some who want people to believe that they themselves [men-at-arms] would never commit such wicked deeds [seizing people and goods without justification], for they have them done by their own men."[27]

There is only one valet who appears in the *Questions on War*, and he seems to truly be a marginal figure, trapped between his master and one of his master's peers, charged with doing dangerous duty and failing. A man-at-arms captures another and turns him over to a valet for safekeeping:

> *(W75) Then another... finds the prisoner which the valet of the other companion is guarding and demands from him whose prisoner he is, and the prisoner responds, "So and so of your party." ...the companion says that he will kill him if he does not swear to be his prisoner. And this one takes his oath as a prisoner and takes him away despite the valet.*

One wonders about what the first man-at-arms might say to his valet in such a situation, but it is clear from Charny's formulation of the problem that a valet or other servant is no companion. The second man-at-arms does not even address him.

Many modern students of the Hundred Years War, professional and amateur, have an image of French noble warriors as arrogant and self-absorbed.[28] Certainly the *Questions* provide plenty of material from which to build such a picture. But perhaps we should also admit that a more charitable perspective can be taken. Charny's *Questions*, though they tell us much about practical matters, at the same time are a script for a conversation between companions. If the men-at-arms ignored their servants and auxiliary troops much of the time, those common warriors had their own interests and also their customary perquisites (note the separate pot of booty reserved for footmen in W70.). They too were companions—of each other—but since they had no personal standing under the law of arms as understood by men-at-arms, Charny had no interest in saying much about them.

Endnotes

1. The term *gens de guerre* does not appear in the body of the ordinance or in Charny's writings.
2. A final goal was to establish military units of sufficient size and of sufficient organization so that commanders of small and medium-sized units would know their men and be responsible for them.
3. Text in *Ordonnances des Roys de France*, IV, 67–70; trans. in large part *in Society at War: the experience of England and France during the Hundred Years War*, ed. C.T. Allmand (Edinburgh: Oliver & Boyd, 1973), 45–8.
4. Wright, 9–10, 57–8.
5. See Andrew Ayton and J.L. Price, eds., *The Medieval Military Revolution State, Society and Military Change in Medieval and Early Modern Europe* (London and New York: I.B. Tauris, 1995); Clifford J. Rogers, ed., *The Military Revolution Debate: Readings on the Military Transformation of Early Modern Europe* (Boulder, Colo. : Westview Press, 1995).

6. Ayton, *Knights and Warhorses : Military Service and the English Aristocracy under Edward III* (Woodbridge: Boydell Press, 1994); Contamine, *Guerre,* 17–22.
7. For instance, see Sumption 2:242, 246 on the role of cavalry at Poitiers.
8. Kaeuper and Kennedy, 177.
9. Kaeuper, *Holy Warriors: the Religious Ideology of Chivalry* (Philadelphia : University of Pennsylvania Press, 2009), 135–44 on labor as a key chivalric attribute.
10. The ordinance for the Crusading fleet sailing to Lisbon in 1147 forbade anyone "to retain the seaman or servant of another in his employ;" Allen and Amt, 305. The parallel to T1, 2, 3, and 21 is noteworthy, even though the retainers in the *Questions* are all men-at-arms.
11. W47, 48, 54, 55, 57.
12. W80A.
13. Keen, *Laws of War,* 35, citing an English arbitration of 1359.
14. For the role of heralds in the 15th century, see Muhlberger, *Deeds of Arms,* 9 n. 33; Keen, *Laws of War,* 254–7; the role of the Parlement of Paris in the later decades of the hundred years war was so extensive that it provided many of Keen's most useful examples of the law of arms in action.
15. W80A seems to show disgruntled captives petitioning the captain of their captor to release them from their obligations as prisoners, exactly the procedure one would expect from Keen's survey; but is this Charny writing? Even if it is, this one instance is hardly a ringing endorsement of the captain's authority over his troops, or as an independent interpreter of the law of arms. Note also that Charny deemphasizes the role of the captain in taking booty as described in Keen's book so that it seems that the disputes are entirely arguments between men-at-arms; yet W50 in passing shows the role of the captain.
16. Froissart 14:106. My translation, based on Johnes'.
17. Contamine shows that "companions" was also used to describe groups of common soldiers.
18. For instance, in W2 reference is made to knights and squires under a lord and not men-at-arms.
19. The other appearance of the term is in W54, where a gentleman without a horse has to take a contract as a foot sergeant.
20. The many meanings of sergeant can be seen under "sergent" in *the Dictionnaire du Moyen Français (1330–1500)* at ATILF (http://atilf.atilf.fr/dmf, accessed January 16, 2014).
21. See the case of John Kingston, discussed above at n. 110.
22. It is clear from the wording of the question that all of the warriors concerned started out on horseback, since "the captain orders that all should dismount to fight on foot."
23. See W38, in which men-at-arms who refuse to fight on foot ask for compensation for mounts lost during a battle. Both cowardice and the unwillingness to appear as a coward were major concerns in medieval warfare: Steven Morrillo "Expecting Cowardice: Medieval Battle Tactics Reconsidered," *Journal of Medieval Military History* 4 (2006), 65–73; Andrew Taylor, "Chivalric Conversation and the Denial of Male Fear." *Conflicted Identities and Multiple Masculinities: Men in the Medieval West.* Ed. Jacqueline Murray (Garland Press: 1999) 169–88.
24. Paris : Mouton, 1972, 65–8.
25. Contamine, *Guerre,* 65–74.
26. Wright, 9–10, 89–90.
27. Kaeuper and Kennedy, 179.
28. See the Shakespearian satire on the vain French nobility debating armor and horses in *Henry V,* 3.7.

5 WHAT MEN-AT-ARMS WORRIED ABOUT

Since Charny provided us with no answers to the *Questions on War*, the best use we can make of them is to search for what some party or another considered to be the most vital issues facing those involved with the law of arms. Interested parties are easy to identify. Geoffroi de Charny took responsibility for every question: They all begin *Je demande* or *Charny demande*. His patron the king supported this initiative, and he and other royal advisers may have had an active role in composing the list. The guiding idea shared by Charny and other possible contributors to the list was that knowledge of the law of arms was the concern of knights, squires and men-at-arms. On one hand, the *Questions* reflected the kind of information that men-at-arms might need to defend themselves in certain kinds of disputes. On the other hand they also represent the kind of knowledge that men-at-arms would need to apply the law of arms, as judges, as advisors of judges, or as arbitrators. Remember that the targeted audience was not just any set of men-at-arms. They as members of the Order of the Star were an elite group chosen by the king for their talents, experience, or potential as leaders and participants in war. If the king valued them so highly, they would qualify as "knights and squires of standing"—a phrase used to describe arbitrators in a case about booty adjudicated under the law of arms in 1359.[1] The *Questions on War*, by addressing prominent French men-at-arms both in their role as potential litigants and as legal authorities, provide us with a picture of the legal issues that caused the most anxiety among warriors of gentle status.

We already know that these legal issues almost never involved inferior members of the armies in which men-at-arms fought. It is not that Charny and his peers did not care about sergeants, valets, archers and the like; it is simply that disciplining common warriors did not pose a difficult problem, at least in theory. Routine discipline was defined by ordinances issued by the commanding officer. The commander may have faced practical difficulties in regulating the riotous behavior of common soldiers, but in principle his authority was undoubted; and certainly he would receive backing from other men-at-arms. More complex were those disputes where a man whose status was doubtful would infringe on the privileges of gentlemen. Thus such questions as W54, 69, and 70 would necessarily involve discussion of the law of arms; such cases might well engender unusual interest among men-at-arms.

Matters of discipline involving the relationship of men-at-arms with their captains are also seldom discussed. As a result, there are only a few places in the *Questions on War* where something really resembling modern military science, or practical matters of military organization, are presented as worthwhile topics for discussion. In one case, the arrangements of lodging within the host cause a confrontation between two men-at-arms, men holding the important office of constable, and each leading sizable retinues:

> *(W26) It happens that the captain has one of his salaried constables*[2] *leave, and this constable has a good fifty men-at-arms under his banner, and they are all sent to be the garrison to defend a city of the said captain; ... another hired foreign constable joins the army and*

> *he has as many men-at-arms as the one who has left, and he lodges in the quarters of the one who has left by the orders of the marshal of the army. It happens that the captain of the army orders the constable who left to return. So he returns to the army, and comes to the army under orders to lodge in his original quarters, and the constable whom he finds lodged there refuses to leave. How will it be judged by the law of arms?*

Although the arrangements appear to be the responsibility of their commander, the dispute between men who are social equals and of equivalent importance in the army is presented as a case needing legal adjudication. Question 32 is more interesting. It shows a situation where a captain issues orders through his marshals and constable, the traditional high officers of the army, and those orders actually take effect, moving both horse and foot to a chosen position where they take up guard duty:

> *(W32) A captain with all his army is lodged in the fields or country of his enemy; and when evening comes the constables and the marshal go to set the guard for the horse and the foot; and they show them where they ought to hold themselves and remain.*

Because the constables and marshal did a poor job of arranging the guard, there is a successful night attack through a gap in the camp's defenses. The guardsmen hold their position as ordered, and as a result the attackers do a great deal of damage to the army. The guard is blamed:

> *(W32) And so some say that that if the guard had rescued them, that their enemies would not have got away. Which should be more praised: to remain in their ordained place in the manner described above, or to have come to the rescue of the army in such need as described above? What do you think is better and more honorable?*

Here the *dramatis personae* include an overall commander, his officers, and warriors on horseback and on foot, in other words something resembling a real army, and the issue raised concerns the following of orders. Charny puts the question in such a way that it must be decided by ascertaining which course of action was more honorable, more likely to be generally approved. The law of arms is not mentioned. We cannot be sure how Charny would have answered W32, or wished his audience to answer it, but one gets the distinct impression that an honorable, i.e. successful, course of action was rated more highly than literal obedience to orders. The captain's opinion on this matter might be important, but he is not portrayed as the central, authoritative figure he might be.

Not that captains and lords are insignificant. There was a personal tie and an important one between leaders and followers. Charny shows that one's loyalty to one's leader is expressed in one's willingness to stick close to him. If we are to believe Charny, one of the more difficult dilemmas faced by men-at-arms on the battlefield was whether such tangible expressions of loyalty had a higher priority than other duties. For instance, if one is a bodyguard of a defeated captain, can one justify leaving the battlefield with him, rather than sending him out of the fight and then returning to the fray? (W8) If a man- at-arms acting as a bodyguard sees not one but two of his brothers in danger during a battle, can he honorably leave his captain and lord to save them? (W33) The issue of leaving the battlefield was central to many of the questions, and we have already seen that the Order of the Star had as a central value of its members that one should never run away. Here we see that the personal tie to one's captain, the obligation to defend him, was perhaps as important as the strongly felt obligation to remain on the battlefield to the bitter end.

It would appear, however, that Charny's men-at-arms thought of themselves at least as often as protagonists than as followers under orders. There are four questions that are very reminiscent of Beaumanoir's thirteenth-century compilation of the customs of the Beauvaisis, in which a long discussion of the legalities of war is entirely devoted to defining who can fight a war (*guerre*) and what limitations on violence exist in this state of affairs.[3] Beaumanoir's *guerre* is not war as we usually mean it today, but the privilege of gentle lineages to defend their honor through private, limited war in a local society. For Charny, local wars fell under the law of arms, as it described the rights of men-at-arms. Questions that certainly concern local war (W12, 20, 22, 23) seem to be focused on defining how a good man-at-arms can fulfill his duty to support friends, neighbors and relatives without getting into unnecessary trouble. Questions W22 and W23 treat the obligation to help a close neighbor against someone more distantly connected. If the close neighbor requires you to help defend his house, will you be involved in the war afterwards if you do nothing more but stay in the house? (The immediacy of this question (W22) is signaled by the fact that the man-at-arms on the hotspot is referred to as "you," a unique occurrence.) What if the helpful neighbor ("you") goes beyond stationary defense, and attacks with lance or on horseback, but (by luck?) doesn't do any damage? (W23) "Would he be able to say with reason that he was not at war?" Question W12 discusses the rights of men who have lent their horses to friends, who use them in a war that the horse owners are not involved in. If enemies recognize the horses and go out and seize them, can the owners object that the two groups should be at peace? One of the most complex of all the war questions is W20, where Charny sketches out the efforts of a "powerful man" to manipulate the rules of local war to his advantage. The powerful man has found himself on the losing side and fears to lose his property. He knows that if he were a principal party of this war rather than simply a "helper," many people on the other side would be obliged to fight for him, and so he tries to get himself named as the principal. Legitimate tactic, or not?[4]

Even if we cannot be sure that these questions on local war reflect a living reality, one is sensitized to two issues. First, war in the *Questions* is seldom unambiguously a matter of state policy or royal privilege; even when members of the Order of the Star sat in council before King Jean II, they were more likely to be thinking of war as their natural environment. Further, the dilemmas they faced seem to be very intimate ones, in that what they worried about most was preserving honor and perquisites in difficult situations, where they were being examined and judged, potentially very severely, by men of their own sort.

One of the most important ways that men-at-arms—or other warriors for that matter—benefited from warfare, an expensive and dangerous way of life, was by taking booty. Excluding the cases that concern taking horses in the context of jousting, the *Questions on War* include eighteen cases on booty, and nearly all of them are detailed discussions of who is entitled to take a share of captured property.

There are a number of theoretical issues that could be discussed in connection with plunder. Keen, for instance, cites complex justifications found in later lawyers' treatises about the legitimacy of taking plunder.[5] Charny has little interest in framing the question in this way. There is no doubt expressed or even hinted at about the right to booty in either the *Questions* or the *Book of Chivalry*. Question W9 was composed in complete confidence that booty was a legitimate perquisite. It discusses when and if booty reclaimed from the enemy must be returned to the original owners by friendly warriors who took it back from the plunderers. We know that the later legal doctrine favored those who retook booty if the enemy had held it for long enough.[6] It is not possible from

W9 to figure out whether the first plunderers have held onto it for long enough by that later standard, but it is difficult to imagine Charny disagreeing with the general principle that booty is fair game once it is secured, and generally that civilian victims of war (who make a rare and ghostly appearance here) are out of luck.

The problems of booty were, for Charny, strictly a matter of legitimate division of goods. Maurice Keen, relying on the fifteenth century biography *Le Jouvencel,* identified three different principles of division in the Hundred Years War: *à butin,* in which pillage was divided according to rank; *à prix d'une esguillette,* equal divisions; *à bonne usance,* where every man kept his own gains. In the fifteenth century, which of the three would apply was announced by the captain when the battle seemed won and going after booty was possible.[7] Charny does not use this classification, and seems to know only two alternatives, division by shares (which he refers to by the terms *butin* and *butiner*)[8] or "each one keep[s] the prisoners and other things he happens to get." (W83) He asks the audience in this question which course of action will more likely assure that the men-at-arms are all to profit from a day's fighting. Again no answer, but the way he poses the question, and the fact that he discusses disputes about *butin* tells us which was the more important method and hints at his own attitude. After all, Charny would have been quite capable of creating complex scenarios involving disagreements between two men-at-arms instead of groups, had he cared to.

There was plenty to say about his chosen subject. He devotes eighteen questions to booty, and they continue on with complications of the most delightful or frustrating nature, depending on one's point of view. There are enough hints in these questions to indicate that the captains had an important role in regulating division of booty, but once again Charny obscures their role and presents cases as setting men-at-arms against men-at-arms, who must debate their disagreements. What they argue about is simple. A certain group is entitled, by general agreement or by ordinance laid down by the captain, to share in a given pot of loot. One man-at-arms or a small retinue claim to be qualified to take part, and others object.

A few examples follow. In W47 a man-at-arms—a banneret with ten men-at-arms in his retinue—sets out as part of a larger group to raid the enemy, but gets lost. He and his men return to the city, care for their horses, feed themselves and after this break ride out again. This time he has better luck, and they find and seize a great deal of booty. He is not, however, satisfied with this. When he returns to the city with his profits,

> *...he finds the others in whose company he first set out from the city, who have gained in the same manner a great deal from their enemies. So the companion with the ten men-at-arms demands his share of booty of the companions in whose company he had set out with in the morning and whom he had lost track of. In annoyance the other companions say no.*

Interestingly enough, Charny indicates that it was possible that the banneret might win the case, and that such a victory would encourage further litigation (W48):

> *...the others would also want to demand for the common booty that which the companions gained after they left the city, after the repast that they had in the city. And the companions say no for all the good reasons that are able to be used by one party or the other.*

More annoyance resulted, one suspects.

The tale of the lost banneret and his claim on the larger company's booty is actually one of the simpler disputes about the allocation of the profits of war. Questions W49, 50, and 51 required

Charny's audience to rule on the very complex situation of a man-at-arms, originally part of a garrison, who is required to undertake detached duty by his captain to deal with the supply needs of the garrison and watch over the pillage his side is storing in a city also held by the captain. This man-at-arms is therefore separated from his companions at the castle, who would be the logical sharers of booty with him. Both the man-at-arms and his former companions proceed to gain a great deal of booty, in a battle where all of them fight, but not together (the man-at-arms fights with the captain; the rest of the garrison shows up on its own initiative). How are the shares and qualifications for them to be determined? An ordinance made in the castle (by whom?) says "that none should have a share of booty except those who rode out." Can the man-at-arms' actions be interpreted as riding out with the men at the castle? "Those in the garrison say no." Question W50 draws our attention to the fact that there is another pot of booty which the captain has promised (ordained) will be split by the men who rode out with him on the day of the battle. Is the man-at-arms on detached duty entitled to a share of this pot? Question W51 visualizes a situation where that man-at-arms "takes a share in the booty with his companions of the garrison of the said castle, and also that he takes a share of the booty of the captain of the country," then asks if the members of the castle garrison who rode out can demand shares in the share which the man-at-arms received for fighting with the captain? "The man-at-arms," of course, "says no." We are at least reassured that "many good arguments are given on either side," even if we can't see which eventually might carry the day. If we don't know the answer, we are given a glimpse of the complexities and tensions of camp life, and the divisions that might spring up among "companions" on the same side for reasons that are understandable enough from a practical point of view.

There is also something to be learned from a group of questions that can be summed up with the phrase, "Is it good enough simply to ride out with a company to be included in its division of booty, even if you do nothing else?" Put that way, the answer seems pretty obvious, but it was perhaps not so clear in 1352 to all men-at-arms. At least five questions out of the eighteen on the division of booty involve warriors who put in a claim for a share even though they did not take part in fighting or in acquiring the spoils. In W41 one part of a group of men-at-arms gets separated from the rest, and makes no gains. The other party gains a great deal. When they are reunited, does the first group share the profits, since they set out together "by agreement and in a common undertaking (*emprise*)"? In W42 a group of about one hundred men-at-arms gets accidentally divided into two parties and many of those in one party are captured, while the second party rallies and defeats the enemy. Some of the captives eventually return to camp on parole "and demand a share of the gains." Question W45 shows a similar situation, except the returnees claiming a share of victory are not paroled prisoners but men who left the battlefield when their side appeared to be losing. A captain in W52 has ordered that all booty should be divided, and then is faced with the objections of some of his men to sharing with others who fled the battle. A final example in W55, the case where some men-at-arms refuse to dismount and fight which we looked at in the previous chapter, is similar. The warriors who stayed on horseback were not simply disobedient, they also used their easy mobility to abandon the temporarily dismounted men who won the day.[9] Was Charny belaboring a point? Or were the men-at-arms that he and his comrades in the Order of the Star both exemplified and commanded truly that disorderly and determined to act as free agents whenever it seemed advantageous? The structure and contents of the *Questions on War* argue that the men-at-arms were reluctant to acknowledge even the ordinances of their captains unless they were browbeaten into it by the arguments and opinions of their own companions.

If the thorough discussion of booty illustrates the importance of booty to the individual warrior, Charny's *Questions* indicate that even more central for a man-at-arms was capturing enemies or being captured by them, gaining ransoms or having to pay them. The thirty-three questions that address captivity and ransom are more than a third of the war questions, one quarter of all of Charny's *Questions*. This preponderance is due to the extreme situation that captivity constituted. Taking prisoners and selling them back was potentially a great source of profit, something looked forward to by those who believed in their luck; at the same time, however much being captured was preferable to being killed, captivity was a condition whose horrifying possibilities haunted the members of Charny's audience.

General knowledge of late medieval customs surrounding captivity tend to focus on two high-profile cases where great lords treated their princely prisoners with ostentatious courtesy. After winning the Battle of Poitiers in 1356, Edward Prince of Wales (the "Black Prince"), humbly (?) served the captive King Jean and other ranking French prisoners at dinner:

> *The same day of the battle at night the prince made a supper in his lodging to the French king and to the most part of the great lords that were prisoners... and always the prince served before the king as humbly as he could, and would not sit at the king's board for any desire that the king could make, but he said he was not sufficient to sit at the table with so great a prince as the king was.*[10]

We have also seen that earlier at Calais, Charny got the same luxury treatment from Edward III, though the shame he reportedly felt at being openly taunted by the king shows the limits of courtesy even in such cases.[11] These incidents were exceptional, and were included in Froissart's *Chronicles*. They have been cited endlessly since as examples of sterling noble behavior.

This was not the general model of conditions of captivity. On the theoretical side, scholars in the law were aware that Roman law allowed the winners to enslave the defeated. If reducing the defeated to chattel slavery was not normal or even tolerated in wars between Christians, a generous estimate of the rights of the victor still remained the basis for the treatment of captured warriors.[12] One did not need university degrees in the two laws to be aware of this; after all, if the captive is called a prisoner in Charny's *Questions on War*, his master is called—the master. And although gentlemen warriors may have thought or hoped that the ultimate implications of this terminology was not realized in practice at their expense, there were plenty of examples of bad behavior in contemporary warfare that might make them uneasy. It must have been common knowledge even in northern France that Mediterranean wars between Christians and Muslims were practically financed on both sides by the profits of enslaving warriors and noncombatants who had the misfortune to be captured by "infidels." The slaves in this case were sometimes ransomed by their families or in the case of Christians by charitable organizations that specialized in freeing the captives, but unless and until that happened, they labored hard in grueling conditions and commonly received the harshest mistreatment.[13] And it was not always on the frontiers of Christendom that "masters" were merciless in the treatment of the helpless who just happened to be on the wrong side of a conflict. Practically at the same time Charny was composing his *Questions*, a Breton knight was criticizing an English mercenary for his oppression of the "poor people" of Brittany:

> *Thus the Bretons saw the small folk suffer,*
> *And for them they had great pity.*
> *One was in shackles, another was put in irons,*
> *One in handcuffs and another in dungeon.*

Two by two, three by three, each one was bound
Like cows and oxen which are led to market.
When Beaumanoir saw them his heart sighed,
And this is what he said, with great boldness to Brambroc
"Knights of England, you do great evil,
To torment the poor people, those who sow the grain
And provide the meat and the wine that they raise.
Without such workers nobles would have to labor
In the fields with the flail and the hoe.
They would suffer poverty, and this would be
A great and unaccustomed toil.
Those who have endured so much should have peace
From now on.[14]

The poet's judgment sounds enlightened and chivalrous (at least in the latter term's modern sense), but in all likelihood it is simply a stereotypical critique of the bad guys. The poet says nothing more about his oppressed poor countrymen, who in real life continued to be captured, dragged off, forced into service, and held for ransom for decades to come.

That men-at-arms were supposedly immune from some of the abuse inflicted on the poor was no guarantee that things might not go badly wrong. We see this in an offhand remark of Froissart's, which seemingly out of context condemns what are supposedly typically German practices:

Sir Bertrand du Guesclin (whose entrance into the office of constable had been thus fortunately signalized, in a way to gain him great honor and reputation) came to Paris, accompanied by the lord de Clisson, and bringing with them the greater part of the [English] prisoners, to whom they behaved very handsomely, allowing them to go at large on their parole for their ransom. They neither shut them up in prison, nor put on shackles and fetters, as the Germans do in order to obtain a heavier ransom. Curses on them for it. These people are without pity or honor, and they ought never to receive quarter. The French entertained their prisoners well, and ransomed them courteously without being too hard on them.[15]

One wonders if Froissart was subtly criticizing the English here. The brutal treatment that he has displaced to Germany in this passage is precisely what Charny's audience feared in their own environment, where the English were the foe. Even gentle warriors might suffer worse: in another passage from Froissart not too many years after Charny wrote, there is a story of an argument between the duke of Anjou and the Englishman Sir Robert Knolles, about whether a besieged castle had to be surrendered according to an earlier and possibly defective agreement, which agreement had been secured by the English garrison giving hostages to the French besiegers. When the argument bogged down, it was the captives on either side,[16] who had no recourse, who ended up dead:

When the herald had delivered this answer [in which Knolles refused to abide by the earlier agreement to surrender the fortification], the duke of Anjou sent for the headsman, and ordered the hostages, who were two knights and a squire, to be brought forth, and had them beheaded before the castle, so that those within might see and know them.

> *Sir Robert Knolles instantly ordered a table to be fixed outside of the windows of the castle, and had led there four of his prisoners, three knights and a squire, for whom he might have had great ransom, but he had them beheaded and flung down in the ditch, the heads on one side and the bodies on the other.*
>
> *The siege was raised after this, and all the men-at-arms returned to France.*[17]

These examples of captivity and its dangers do not directly relate to the discussion of ransom in the *Questions on War*; as he did in his discussion of other topics, Charny ignored much of the reality of enslavement or captivity in warfare. His questions reflect the fears of men-at-arms, who did have reason to hope for better treatment. There were fears of two kinds, the first being the fear that a potential "master" might feel, wondering if he might be cheated of his rightful gains by a deceitful prisoner or a rival captor. In W81, a man-at-arms avoids captivity by falsely claiming that he is already the prisoner of another captor, who in fact, has not seen him that day. Stronger, however, was the fear of the same man-at-arms that if captured he would be subjected to an uncompromising and demeaning state of unfreedom. Where the man-at-arms-as-master needed guidance to secure his profits, an anxiety-producing situation, the man-at-arms-as-prisoner visualized some breakdown of the law of arms which would result in him being contemptuously robbed by a greedy master of his few personal luxuries, or being arbitrarily deprived of his freedom to move beyond his quarters, or beaten, or threatened with death (W66, 60, 64, 71).[18] These fears were not unrealistic; the reciprocal benefits of maintaining a working body of customs around the taking of men-at-arms by others were compelling—ransoms and assurance that they would usually be paid kept unlucky men-at-arms alive—but the prisoner was always playing for higher stakes. As a result there are more examples of questions that seem to be from the prisoner's point of view than there are from the master's.

The captivity/ransom cases have a unique status in the *Questions on War*. We know how Frenchmen of later generations answered many of them. Both Bouvet's treatise *The Tree of Battles* and the records of archives in England and France provide us with detailed case studies and often legal rulings. Michael Anthony Taylor and Jean Rossbach in their unpublished editions were able to cross reference several questions with later treatises. Yet we cannot be sure that Bouvet, for instance, gives us answers that would have won wide consent in the ranks of the Order of the Star during a discussion in 1352. Maurice Keen argued persuasively in his *Laws of War* that it was the scale, persistence, and international implications of the Hundred Years War that led to the creation of widely recognized legal doctrines and precedents. Since the *Questions* of 1352 are perhaps the earliest documentation of that long-term collective effort, we cannot read later doctrines back into them, given the lack of direct evidence.

For instance, an important question is whether a warrior who had surrendered could legitimately be rescued and freed, or could take an unexpected opportunity to flee captivity himself. We have a number of different sources that throw some light on this situation: Charny's *Questions,* a literary source contemporary with the *Questions,* an addition to the *Questions* by an unknown annotator, and later legal documentation investigated by Maurice Keen and others. Keen and others have shown from plentiful archival documentation that the bond created when a man-at-arms surrendered was a contract that was inheritable.[19] However, the other sources leave us in our usual uncertainty about what earlier doctrine and practice were.

The anonymous Breton verse account of the Combat of Thirty against Thirty records an arranged deed of arms between French and English garrisons in Brittany, which took place in 1351 and where an escape from custody was a crucial point in the battle. The Combat was interpreted by the Breton poet (and other observers as well) as an admirable exercise of chivalric virtues, carried out by knights and squires who were fighting *a outrance*, that is, until all were captured or dead.[20] The early part of the fight went to the English, whose commander, Brambroc, took three of the Franco-Bretons prisoner. Then Brambroc was killed. His captives reacted immediately:

> *At these words, Charruel is on his feet, and the valiant Tristan,*
> *Who was so badly wounded, and Caro de Bodegat*
> *The preux and the honored. All three were prisoners of*
> *Brambroc the mad,*
> *But when Brambroc was dead they were freed.*
> *Each one took in his hands the good sharp swords.*
> *They have a good will to strike the English.*[21]

There is no hint here that anyone objected to the prisoners rejoining the combat; the poet is clear that his Breton heroes are acting heroically by rejoining the fight. The problem is that the poet's standards of what was fair and legitimate were partisan,[22] and we have no countervailing pro-English version to give a different interpretation.

The *Questions on War* present us with a number of cases where men-at-arms have surrendered and subsequently escape or are rescued. Sometimes there is an obvious justification:

> *(W57) One of the men-at-arms in one party takes one from the other side, and that one surrenders himself as prisoner by his good faith, if the other protects him from death; and the one who takes him promises him and then leaves him unguarded. So it happens that some of the men-at-arms of the same party as he who took the prisoner find this prisoner and tell him that if he does not surrender he will die, and he answers that he has surrendered to one of their party and gives his name. They don't believe him and strike him and wound him in many places and want to kill him if he does not surrender, and during this conflict the prisoner is rescued by his party and is led off to safety. The one who first captured him requires him to come to him as a captive according to the faith which he gave; and the other says that he is not required to do so.*

Sometimes it is not so clear:

> *(W58) One of the parties has the better of it at the beginning, so that those in this party take ten or twelve prisoners. In the end it happens that the party of the prisoners rally and attack the others and defeat them entirely and take possession of the field and recover all the other prisoners taken at the beginning. And so those who took the first prisoners that they should come and be their prisoners; some of those who took the first prisoners are taken themselves and some have gone. It was said to the first prisoners: "Swear to be my prisoner," and so they did it and should not be contesting this captivity. The first say that they are not required to go, and the others say that they are.*

The principle of hereditary ownership of ransom rights was known to Charny, and appears in the following case:

> *(W61) The prisoner comes to his [agreed-upon] place and time with his ransom, but he finds that his master has been dead for some time. So he remains there the whole day;*

and they take him before the heir of his master and demand the money from the prisoner. The prisoner says that he is not required to give it.

Of course, "Many good arguments are given on either side." It seems, however, that at least in the early stages of the capture, prisoners felt justified in (or could not resist) running away if they could. Question 80A, which is attributed to Charny, but which is found only in one manuscript, sketches an interesting and perhaps later case:

(W80A) ...it happens that one of the men-at-arms who has the upper hand takes another man-at-arms and he who is taken surrenders to one who has taken him and gives his faith as his prisoner. But very soon the party of the prisoner has the better of it and defeats the others and takes the field, and the prisoner, who sees his party get the upper hand attacks his enemies and takes two or three of them and makes them swear to be prisoners and gives them a day to return. Those come on their day and demand of the captain of the one to whom they had sworn by the law of arms saying that they should not be held to be prisoners to him who on that day had a prison notwithstanding that he is able to argue that because of the rescue he ought to be free; and the first one taken says that they are his prisoners, for he was rescued.

Some of the questions on the legitimacy of escape also treat the issue of when exactly a prisoner can be said to have actually surrendered and to whom. In one we see a tough man-at-arms apparently making the best choice of future master, in a story reminiscent of one told about William Marshal:[23]

(W56) One of the men-at-arms in one party strikes his spurs to save himself, and three of the other side pursue him. The first stops him with the bridle, and he does not want to surrender to him. The second takes him by the head and holds a knife at his throat, and again he does not wish to surrender to him. The third comes after and tells him to surrender to him, and that man-at-arms surrenders himself to the third. When in the evening each of the three uses all the good arguments he knows, and there are plenty, that this prisoner ought to belong to him. Who will have him, and how will it be judged by the law of arms?

This would seem to be one of the more straightforward questions, especially if surrender is a contract under the law. But in other cases Charny shows that the signal word or deed that indicated a contract had been struck was not clear to every man-at-arms. Maurice Keen concluded from his reading of documents that at some point there was a standard, namely "he should be the first man to seize the prisoner's right gauntlet and to put his right hand in his."[24] Curiously, this later standard makes no appearance in Charny's *Questions on War*; rather legal questions hung on the words used to surrender, and whether saying "I surrender to you [*Je me rent a toi*]" was as definitive as "giving faith [*bailler sa foy*]" in establishing a firm contract. Question W75 focuses on some of the issues surrounding the act of surrender:

(W75) Men-at-arms encounter each other and fight until one of the parties is defeated. It happens that one man-at-arms of the party with the upper hand takes a man-at-arms of the defeated party and says to him, "Surrender to me!" And the man-at-arms says "I surrender to you," and gives him his sword; and the one who has captured him gives him to one of his valets to guard and this companion goes to fight with the others. Then

> *another of those who have the upper hand comes and finds the prisoner which the valet of the other companion is guarding and demands from him whose prisoner he is, and the prisoner responds, "So and so of your party." The man-at-arms asks if he has given his faith, and the prisoner replies that he has not given any faith, at which the companion says that he will kill him if he does not swear to be his prisoner. And this one takes his oath as a prisoner and takes him away despite the valet. And when evening comes the companion who first took him without faith being pledged demands his prisoner; the other who has his faith says no. Many good arguments are given on either side. How will it be judged by judgment of arms?*

A number of points could be argued here, in particular whether the presence of a servant who lacked personal authority was a sufficient provision by the captor of protection for the vulnerable prisoner.[25] But the case does seem to hang on whether the first captor's claim is less valid because he did not receive or ask for an explicit expression of good faith.[26] Unfortunately, but all too typically, Charny does not give his audience an explicit and precise example of "giving one's faith," nor is he clear on the issue of whether giving faith is even necessary if one has surrendered. We simply have his word that good (or at least probable) arguments could be advanced on either side.

Such arguments grew out of competing interests and competing anxieties. The motivation for captives to cheat their would-be masters was very strong. If one could run away before the captor had secured his hold, the captive man-at-arms might hope to escape imprisonment, possible abuse, and the devastating consequences of paying a huge ransom. Running away might even be a necessity, at least as the prisoner told the story later; remember W57, where the unguarded man-at-arms was threatened with death. In other cases, however, the prisoners seem to be exploiting the uncertainties of contemporary practice:

> *(W58)... It was said to the first prisoners: "Swear to be my prisoner," and so they did it and should not be contesting this captivity. The first say that they are not required to go...*
>
> *(W59) A prisoner is taken in the field... and it is required that he swear to be a prisoner and he does it. And [the captor]... puts him under guard without asking any other oath. And [the prisoner] escapes the next day and gets himself to safety. Can he do this without reproach?*
>
> *(W67) ... No one asks for him to pledge faith and he does not give it. And the one who is taken looks over the field, sees his advantage, and strikes his spurs and thus goes his way. Tell me if he is able to do this without reproach... ?*
>
> *(W81) A man-at-arms takes another in a set battle and tells him, "Surrender," and the other answers, "I won't because I am the prisoner of such and such," and gives a name. And the one who arrested him says, "Give me your faith that you are the prisoner of the one you name," and the other gives his faith that such is the case, and the other frees him. When evening comes that one [i.e. the captor] who knows that he was the prisoner of the other speaks to him [i.e. the first supposed captor] and this one, who knows nothing of it, nor has taken the prisoner, nor even seen him during the whole day, says he would like to claim him as his prisoner, and so he does it. And the prisoner says no and that he only did it to save himself. Many good arguments are given on one side or another.*

Any of these, not just the last, might be seen as sharp practice from people on the other side of the dispute, and Charny's *Questions* contain some harsh actions inflicted on men-at-arms whose words of surrender are not necessarily believed. These include cases we have seen before: the prisoner stolen from his initial captor even as a valet stands guard over him (W75), and the prisoner who is killed even though his captor is present and asserting his claim (W80). We are not told in W82 why one man-at-arms does not believe another when he states that cannot surrender because he is the prisoner of "such and such of your party," but after we have read that far we are not surprised to find the would-be captor expressing skepticism at his enemy's declaration and threatening him with death if he continues to refuse to surrender. We can if we wish attribute apparently arbitrary actions on the part of masters to cruelty, greed, and arrogance,[27] but the very existence of the *Questions* and the numerous cases concerning ransom requires us to consider how anxiety about securing gains, doubts about legal doctrines, fears of being cheated by fast-talking barracks lawyers and anger generated by a frustrated sense of entitlement all would contribute to some of the harsh behavior sketched out by Charny. Consider the state of mind of the man-at-arms who saw his prisoner cut down in front of him:

> *(W80) The next day the one who has captured the prisoner takes the one who killed him as his prisoner and takes him without any further defiance and puts him to ransom for as much as he can. And the other says as an excuse that the first cannot take him or ransom him in this manner, while the one who has taken him says he will do it.*

Once again we see the fragility of the law of arms and good reason for it to evolve beyond such do-it-yourself law enforcement. "How will it be judged by the law of arms?" was a pressing question indeed, and we begin to understand why King Jean might want its principles debated before him. Despite the kinds of disagreements described by Charny, there was a common interest among all men-at-arms, among all respectable gentleman warriors that the system—the law of arms—should work to preserve both their gains in war and their legitimate rights to be treated fairly and with respect if taken prisoner. After all, it was the prospect of gain that motivated masters to preserve the life of a captive, while respectful treatment was a mark of the mutual recognition of status that constituted gentle birth with all of its advantages. What we don't know is how developed the doctrines that protected these privileges were. If we remember the coincidence of the ordinance with the *Questions*, we may think that we have a pretty convincing argument that the *chevalerie* of France was extremely self-willed in its own dealings with each other. That Charny's remedy of this state of affairs—or King Jean's remedy—attempted to fix this situation not through an assertion of royal authority, but by appealing explicitly to the right and capability of all men-at-arms to find the proper answers to legal conundrums becomes an interesting fact in itself.

Endnotes

1. My translation of the phrase found at Keen, *Laws of War*, 35: *chivalers et esquiers de valu.*
2. It's apparently worth knowing that the constable is being paid (under contract) but it is not clear what effect this would have on the case.
3. Beaumanoir, 2:354–66. The title of this section in the sole English translation (*The Coutumes de Beauvaisis of Philippe de Beaumanoir*, trans. F.R.P Akehurst (Philadelphia: University of Pennsylvania Press, 1992), 610) is "private war," but in French the title is *Guerre*, and no other kind of war is discussed.
4. The last line of W20 suggests that Charny had an answer: "what ought to be done by the law of arms... for by the custom of the country the chief can be chosen from among the helpers as much as from the captains."
5. Keen, *Laws of War*, 137–55.

6. Charny's questions visualize the first plunderers taking the booty "a good six leagues in peace," while legal documents cited by Keen specify that "an owner lost his title to goods which remained in enemy hands for over twenty-four hours." This from a French case of 1430; Keen, *Laws of War,* 143.
7. Keen, *Laws of War,* 153.
8. *Butiner* has the sense of collecting prizes of war into a common fund to be divided among certain qualified warriors; *butin* indicates the prizes to be so divided, the process of dividing them, the formula used, etc. Generally the actual pillaged objects and beasts were auctioned off and the funds raised were divided; Keen, *Laws of War,* 146–8, 152–4.
9. Whether the mounted men fled or just refused to engage is not possible to say. See also W38.
10. Froissart 5:460–1; Johnes 1:226.
11. See above at n. 12.
12. Keen, *Laws of War,* 156–7, 162 and n. 3–4 refers to lawyers using the term "slaves."
13. A recent treatment: Jarbel Rodriguez, *Captives and their Saviors in the Medieval Crown of Aragon* (Washington, D.C.: Catholic University of America Press, 2007).

14. Brush, 84; my translation.
15. Froissart 8:54; Johnes 1:457–8.
16. Some of the captives here were hostages and not prisoners in the sense we have been discussing, but they were all men-at-arms under the control of other men-at-arms.
17. Johnes, 1:499, a loose translation of Froissart 8: 296–8.
18. The one murdered prisoner (W80) has no standing in court, but is simply a piece of property which one man-at-arms has been deprived of by another. See Richard II's ordinance XIII in the appendix below.
19. Keen, *Laws of War,* 159.
20. Muhlberger, *Deeds of Arms,* 76–111; "The Combat of the Thirty against Thirty: an example of medieval chivalry?" in L.J. Andrew Villalon and Donald J. Kagay, eds., *The Hundred Years War (Part II): Different vistas* (Leiden and Boston: Brill, 2008), 283–94; Will McLean, "*Outrance* and *Plaisance*," *Journal of Medieval Military History* 8 (2010): 155–170.
21. Brush (see n. 110), 106; my translation.
22. Muhlberger, "The Combat of the Thirty against Thirty," 289–93; *Deeds of Arms,* 87–94.
23. *History of William Marshal,* ed. A.J. Holden, S. Gregory & D. Crouch, 3 vols., ANTS Occasional Publications 4–6 (London: Anglo-Norman Text Society, 2002–6) 1:204–5 in which French tourneyers surrendered to William Marshal, alone, instead of the numerous opponents who were on the verge of capturing them. They expected more generous treatment from him and received it.
24. Keen, *Laws of War,* 165–6, and 166 n. 1, a definition derived from Richard II's Durham ordinances and French cases in Parlement and in *Le Jouvencel.*
25. W80 shows a case where a prisoner is killed on the battlefield by a man-at-arms who does not believe that another man-at-arms has already captured him—despite the presence of the first captor and his explicit claim.
26. What might it be? Charny doesn't say.
27. W64 shows motiveless anger; other questions (W63, 66, 71, 72) show mistreatment, threats, or bad faith seemingly aimed at extorting money.

6 HONOR AND THE LORE OF CHIVALRY

Most of the questions we have discussed so far have concerned concrete rights to gains from warfare, or the possession of certain privileges in the making of war. We have already seen, though, that some of the war questions do not refer to the law of arms. Two groups of questions are of particular interest to us.

First, the larger group consists of those which concern "honor." They are not specifically related to the law of arms and are not presented as matters that "should be judged by the law of arms," or "decided by men-at-arms." They are questions which ask Charny's audience to judge whether a given behavior is honorable, or which of two possible behaviors is more honorable. Rather than being asked about the law of arms, those being consulted are being asked about what might be a much more diffuse standard of proper behavior. Some of these questions fit modern ideas of honor, while a few concern what I would call military science, but which Charny discusses in terms of honorable behavior.

Second, there are questions that seem to be chivalric trivia. They ask the respondents to clarify the terminology of chivalry; they ask seemingly hypothetical questions about values and behavior; they sometimes set puzzles that may have been devised for the fun of debating them. Yet even the oddest ones must have meant something to Charny's contemporaries, and their curiosity has the virtue of reminding us of our distance from the subject matter.

Although the term honor is for most people strongly associated with the nobility of the Middle Ages, and although honor is a classic topic in modern anthropology, it is not easy to define.[1] Rather than trying to come up with a global definition, it is simpler and more logical to look at Charny's uses of the appropriate words: honor, honorable, and their antonyms. An examination of his *Book of Chivalry* is particularly useful because those words come up frequently in a context where Charny is not floating provocative questions, but teaching the essence of *armes* and honor. The entire *Book of Chivalry* is about honor, what it really is, and how one achieves it. "Honor" and related words in the *Book of Chivalry* overwhelmingly concern the respect, reputation, and status that a good man-at-arms acquires through military activity.

There are some exceptions to this. Honor also seems to designate the respect that goes along with wealth and inherited status. This kind of family honor, which would seem to be fairly solid as such things go, can be lost or nullified by the attacks of ruthless enemies.[2] Early in the book Charny mentions, in connection with worthy participation in local wars, that it is appropriate for good men-at-arms to fight "in order to defend... their honor and inheritance"[3] or "to assist in the defense of the honor and inheritance of their kinsmen, [or of] their rightful lord who maintains them..."[4] A good man-at-arms' honorable position in society can also be destroyed by his own foolish overindulgence in unworthy amusements. Charny contrasts gambling games characteristic of lowlifes to more noble pleasures: "such pastimes [as jousting, conversation, dancing and singing in the company of ladies and damsels] ...are finer and more honorable and can bring more benefits than can games of dice through which one can lose one's possessions and one's honor and all good company."[5] Thus honor is connected both to one's wealth and by implication to one's social standing.

Honor can also mean the respect due to others of rank and reputation, and showing such respect makes one more honorable, too. Ladies are sources of honor, since to love such a one "truly and honorably [secretly so as not to harm the good standing of either lover]... is the right position to be in for those who desire to achieve [martial] honor."[6] Charny also encourages those who wish to achieve martial honor themselves to show the appropriate honor (respect) to the great men, and even those of middling rank, who have achieved great worth already.[7]

Far more often, however, Charny uses the term to mean "military achievement that leads to higher status or reputation," or occasionally "military effectiveness." Recall that Charny's three books all treat the life of arms as an ascent from the least difficult to the most difficult, and in his most developed presentation of this argument in the *Book of Chivalry*, he shows the life of arms as an ascent from one type of honor or honorable achievement to greater honor associated with more difficult challenges:

> *When **God by his grace grants [aspirant men-at-arms] frequent success in jousting,** they enjoy it, and their desire to bear arms increases. Then after jousting, they learn about the practice of arms in tournaments, and it becomes apparent to them and they recognize that tournaments **bring greater honor** than jousting for those who perform well there. Then they set out to bear arms in tournaments as often as they can... Their knowledge increases until they see and recognize that the men-at-arms who are good in war are **more highly prized and honored** than any other men-at-arms. It therefore seems to them from their own observation that they should immediately take up the practice of arms in war and in order to **achieve the highest honor in prowess,** for they cannot attain this by any other form of armed combat.*[8]

In that passage we see honor as, first, something that is given to worthy men-at-arms by those who recognize their worth; second, as something which is gained by those who strive for it; and third, as something that derives ultimately from God. Honor can also refer to military effectiveness, or the success that comes in warfare to those who "learn the true way to practice the military arms until they, on every occasion, know how to strive towards the most honorable course of action, whether in relation to deeds of arms in relation to other forms of behavior appropriate to their rank."[9] All of these usages of honor have a close direct connection to skill, courage, and success in combat, and it is such usages that dominate the *Book of Chivalry*.

"Dishonor" and the like are used very infrequently in the *Book of Chivalry*. In one case it refers to the potential actions of enemies who attack worthy men and "who come there to kill, disinherit, or dishonor them, if they can, and to take everything from them if they have the power."[10] This and a few similar passages[11] emphasize that the loss of honor, the loss of the ability to uphold one's proper station through poverty or defeat or disgrace, leaves the dishonored one—and his lineage as well—with nothing. Charny also refers to dishonor in connection with the loss of reputation through one's own unworthy actions; he gives two examples of those who in the conduct of war go against honor and therefore lose it. First are those who fight for unworthy reasons, "who take up arms, but are not men-at-arms... because of their very dishonest and disordered behavior under these arms,... those who use arms in this dishonorable way behave like cowards and traitors, nor would they dare to bear arms in any other way."[12] He states elsewhere that one can bring disgrace and dishonor upon oneself in warfare by "falling into too great despair [which] can make a man lose his position and his honor...; but when one is engaged on an armed enterprise one should dread vile cowardice more than death."[13] Although Charny was constitutionally inclined to praise men-at-arms as practitioners of an extraordinarily worthy way of life, and loathe to criticize them, we see him here admitting that it was possible to do great evil under arms, and thoroughly betray the order of chivalry by defaulting on one's duty. The appropriate consequence for such behaviors was or should be the loss of one's respectable position in society. Those in this position are cowards or no better than cowards, even if some of the latter are condemned not for running away but for acting like bandits.

As we turn to what the *Questions on War* say about honor and dishonor, it is worth keeping in mind the seriousness of falling short in one's duty—not so much one's duty to King and Country, which hardly figure in Charny's frame of reference in any explicit way, but one's duty to the life of arms and the law of arms which regulated and justified it.[14] To see oneself and to have others see you as honorable were not just matters of self-esteem, though self-esteem was very important in motivating warriors to undertake dangerous deeds.[15] Honor was a vital part of one's social identity, with practical consequences. Among other things, honor was that which separated the man-at-arms, the gentleman, from the sergeant or the valet or the footman, and gave him access to privileges that these lesser men, who were technically servants, could not enjoy. Charny's *Questions* indicate, for instance, that a sergeant really had no right to take a gentleman prisoner; a valet had no right to impede a gentleman determined to take away a prisoner from his custody; that footmen, even if they had access to a share of an army's profits, had a subordinate claim. The very terminology of the time created doubt whether those who were not called men-at-arms were "real" warriors at all—and led contemporaries to conclude that they necessarily had crass and dishonorable motives: again, they were "men who take up arms, but are not men-at-arms... who want to wage war without good reason."[16] The gentleman warriors, the men-at-arms, were morally better than this (they told each other); [17] and thus they were entitled to the advantages and jurisdiction that they enjoyed over the other denizens of the battlefield and the military camp.

If protecting one's honor was protecting one's claim to preferential access to profit, it was also protecting one's qualification for honorable, that is respectful, treatment; and this was no small thing. The fear shown in W60, 64, and 66, the captive's fear of being beaten, robbed, or just locked up, was the fear of losing one's place in respectable society and of being treated in an entirely arbitrary way—as lesser men sometimes were. Whatever the law of arms said about the treatment of prisoners, or what some of Charny's audience might have said about any particular case, such things went much deeper than any codified formula, into the territory of taboo. Gentlemen felt strongly that gentlemen should enjoy certain basic privileges that mitigated the dangers of warfare. That principle was the foundation of much of Charny's discussion. Charny naturally enough included matters not justiciable, questions that allowed one to establish limits on honorable behavior which among other things, signaled that the people in question were worthy members of the informal cabal of gentlemen who made the rules, who legitimately waged war, who were not random people who had had the misfortune to wander into the path of an army. Similarly Charny touched upon how bad behavior might endanger one's standing in that group.

A burning question that Charny felt obliged to address springs from King Jean's agenda in creating the Order of the Star in the first place. One of the chief goals the king was attempting to accomplish through the order was to revive the formerly sterling quality of French chivalry which had after many centuries fallen grievously, with "some of the members of this order unaccustomed to arms and deprived of exercises, or for some other cause unknown to us [...] immoderately plung[ing] themselves into the idleness and vanity of the age, to the contempt of honor, alas, and of their own good renown." The order was meant to encourage and validate deeds of arms, and deeds of arms of war rather than deeds of arms of peace. The need to shore up the French reputation for valor is indicated by the oath that Jean Le Bel says the members took, "that they would never flee in battle farther than four *arpents* (in their opinion) but would die or surrender."[18] Crécy, the great defeat of Philip VI's time, had thrown a pall of cowardice over the standing of the French military class. There are strong indications in the *Questions on War* that this came down to a simple understanding that too many men-at-arms were too willing to run away from danger instead of fighting their hardest.

Scenarios involving retreating or surrendering or both appear in a conservative estimate in eleven of Charny's questions on war. It is clear from several of them that anything resembling running away might be interpreted as blameworthy. Thus this question:

> *(W30) There is a battle ... in which many men-at-arms of the defeated party depart and go away. Some consider that these have gone on their honor without being defeated; and many others consider that those who have gone are defeated. How can this be?*

Judgments vary, but elsewhere we see that if the judgment was adverse, if one was thought to have been "fleeing" to one's "dishonor," it was so serious that some might think it would wipe out a lifetime of renown (W39). What distinguished dishonorable flight from the "safe and honorable withdrawal" which Charny thought all good men-at-arms needed to learn to execute?[19] Of course we have no correct answer to this, just indications about how serious the dilemma was. For instance, in W31 we have a story that shows what problems arise when good military practice and the perception that one is fleeing conflict:

> *(W31) A captain of men-at-arms rides out in the field and orders some of his scouts to see the situation of his enemies who are in the field; and these scouts are among the more capable of his people. And at the approach of their enemies one party of their enemies pursues them faster than they can go; and the scouts retreat from their enemies and are able to retreat without loss. So there are some of the scouts who turn back and meet their enemies, and perform arms like good people should; and others retreat to their captain and make their report. Which of these are to be more valued and praised: those who went back to their lord or those who are captured?*

The scouts who turn back and fight are doing something good and praiseworthy; yet Charny thought that the scouts who returned were also doing something valuable, and were obedient to their captain to boot. Perhaps Charny anticipated a reflexive endorsement of warriors who "perform arms like good people should." This is consistent with scenarios discussed in W7 and W8, where what might seem sensible course of action is contrasted with conventional belligerent courage. In the first we see a captain, the principal leader of one side in a hypothetical war, who

> *(W7) is defeated but remains on the field so long that he sees and understands that he is unable to recover his fortunes or the day; and the battle has been very well fought. Which is the better thing for him to do: remain and take his chances, or leave so that he can recoup? And if he leaves, should he thereby lose his honor?*

We may think that it hardly makes sense that the captain should sacrifice his rights and his person after one serious defeat; and we've seen that Charny did not reject the possibility of honorable retreat.[20] Then we remember that King Jean refused to leave the field at Poitiers in 1356, even though he understood that the day was lost. This gives the scenario in question W7 a real piquancy. Question W7 also prepares us for the dilemma of the bodyguards in the next question who seriously contemplate abandoning their lord to return to fight in a lost battle. There are good reasons for them to remain with the captain, yet they hesitate (my emphasis):

> *(W8) Which is the better thing to do: lead their master to safety, and in that case, either go with him, or send him outside of the melee alone, and tell him to save himself if he is able?* ***There is a great risk that he will not be able to save himself; and by returning into the battle they take the risk of death or capture. Since they have agreed to be men in his retinue****, will they be blamed if they go with him? Which is better, to go or to stay?*

Neither avoiding the presumed shame of abandoning their employer, their "master," nor the danger of returning to a hopeless situation are unquestionably preferable to the criticism they might attract for leaving the field. Even if we guess that Charny might have a clear preference himself, he expected debate. This is confirmed by other scenarios, which show that there was an entire terminology of warfare, which was meant among other things to clarify what was honorable behavior. One of the questions I would most like answered, were that possible, is this:

> *(W37) I have heard it said that one is able to leave and retreat* (retraire) *from a battle from the defeated side* (la part desconfite)*, if he has acted in seven ways without being killed or taken, without being reproached. How can this be and what are the seven ways?*

It would certainly be very illuminating to have Charny's list of seven mitigating circumstances, and his comments on them, given that he was twice captured and must have twice surrendered himself, even though he did not consider this something that could be done lightly (W79). Unless Charny is disingenuously preparing to present a list of his own as something he heard from others, the list of seven implies a history of serious discussion, perhaps long debate, that unfortunately never found the pen to write it down.

There was also debate about defeat, and when it took place, as seen in this pair of curious questions:

> *(W28) There is a battle between two captains in which one party is defeated and many of the party are dead, concerning whom some say that some of those who are dead are not dead but defeated; and many other say of those who are dead that they are dead and defeated. How can this be?*
>
> *(W29) There is a battle as above in which there are many captured, concerning whom some say that although they are captured, they do not regard them as defeated; and there are many others who consider that those who are taken are defeated as well as captured. How can this be?*

I interpret these questions to mean that the idea of being defeated, *desconfit,* was so unwelcome that even the dead would reject it. We can easily imagine that being called "defeated" stung, but that may underestimate the force of the word. *Desconfit* could mean defeated in some neutral sense, as we find in some passages of the *Book of Chivalry*, but it could mean much more. One relevant but general sense means "destroyed, broken, ruined, reduced to nothingness." There is an old and more specific military sense in which *desconfit* means "routed," a concept of both moral and practical significance for horsemen. Given the existence of different meanings for this loaded adjective, there would be room for disagreement about who could be called *desconfit* and how bad that label might be. (Cf. W30) Was it a state worse than death? Certainly the perception that one had run away in a fearful or undisciplined manner, would seem to open a man-at-arms to this accusation of deepest dishonor.

We are seeing here traces of a special language to describe aspects of war, the fossilized remains of many informal discussions about who did what and whether it was justified. Questions W13-16 gives us some indication of the terminology surrounding different kinds of "combat in the field," which, Charny says, come in three types, *rencontre, besoigne,* and *bataille* (W13). As elsewhere, however, Charny's case studies confuse as much as they clarify. From other sources of the period we can be reasonably sure a *rencontre* was an encounter between two moving armies, or an attack by one side or another; but W13 tells us that "some say that a *rencontre* takes place between a thousand men-at-arms or more on one side and the other." The question further implies that a fight that ends decisively in possession of the field by one side might not be called either a *besoigne* (affair) or a *bataille* (battle); "how should it be designated then?" A good question, whose resolution is not helped by W14, which discusses a combat of more than a thousand men which is ended either by one side taking possession of the field, or by nightfall, two endings which seem inconsistent and imply different degrees of decisiveness. Some believe, says Charny, that since nightfall ended the action, the fight can be "nothing but an affair," and qualifies for neither of the other descriptions. There are enough seeming contradictions in the question that we can't be sure whether they who said this were right.

Nevertheless, we might feel that we are close defining two of the three terms—and able to guess what a *bataille* might be—except that with W16 Charny once again confuses things:

> *(W16) Two captains are in the field to fight and there is a great number of men-at-arms on either side. And so one of the captains and his people are defeated. And the other captain who has overcome him has killed his people, taken a great number of the defeated and gained horses and plenty of other goods. And when the evening comes none consider this to be an encounter, an affair, or a battle. How can this be and what should it be called?*

No doubt Charny had a clever and instructive reason for posing this puzzle, but we are not in a good position to resolve how there could be a decisive conflict in the field that does not fall into one of three categories if, as Charny said earlier, there are only three categories.

If a solid understanding of the terminology of battles remains beyond our grasp, it is reasonably clear that men-at-arms categorized them in part to establish claims to renown, based on participation in different kinds of combat.[21] Maurice Keen cites a similar phenomenon revealed in the testimony given in connection with the famous English heraldry case Scrope v. Grosvenor, where he states "there is a strong impression given of a kind of pecking order distinguishing different levels of martial experience in terms of honor. Robert, Lord Morley, a series of witnesses declared, was especially respected because he had been present at so many 'mortal battles.'" Another witness, Sir Hugh Browe, found it necessary to admit that despite significant experience he had never served "in the great expeditions of war."[22] A well-known story about the battle of Poitiers shows an experienced and capable English commander, Lord James Audley, thinking in quite similar terms, even though, like the other Englishmen, he does not use Charny's categories. According to Froissart's *Chronicles,* Audley was responsible for arranging the battle lines for Edward Prince of Wales. Once he had finished his task, Audley approached the Prince with a request that had to do with his own honor.

> *Sir, I have ever served most loyally my lord your father, and yourself, and shall continue so to do, as long as I have life. Dear sir, I must now acquaint you, that formerly I made a vow, if ever I should be engaged in any battle (*besoigne*) where the king your father or any of his sons were, that I would be the foremost in the attack, and the best combatant on his side, or die in the attempt. I beg therefore most earnestly, as a reward for any services I may have done, that you would grant me permission honorably to quit you, that I may post myself in such wise to accomplish my vow.*[23]

Froissart shows Audley using the least precise and most colorless word for a combat, but despite this the moment is a highly charged one. A man whose experience and practical knowledge of warfare must have been extensive is obsessed by a lack in his career, and feels compelled to take advantage of this opportunity to win renown—a renown that would be certified in the eyes of the world by the testimony of royal princes, who could confirm Audley's individual prowess on a unique occasion. (Like some of Charny's knights, Audley finds the demands of honor pull him away from direct service to his lord; he must ask for permission to take on this challenge.)[24] Audley believed that participation in different kinds of combats increased one's honor in different ways—and that his personal performance had a unique significance. On these points Charny would have been in complete agreement. Charny's favorite catchphrase, after all, was "he who does more is worth more." We see the same emphasis on the individual in *Questions* W78 and 79, except they speak of losing honor and not on gaining it:

> *(W78) Since some contend that when a man-at-arms who is captured in the field, armed in an affair (*besoigne*) and the man-at-arms says "I surrender" or gives his faith, that this ought to be a reproach of cowardice to him, how can he be captured and keep his honor and without reproach?*
>
> *(W79) Since I do not understand when a man-at-arms surrenders himself into the hands of his enemies in a* besoigne *arrestee in what way he can say the words, "I surrender," which will not be considered cowardice, I ask to be enlightened, for I don't understand it.*

The first of these usages of *besoigne* may have been meant as a neutral term for any kind of conflict—*besoigne* is a word with many meanings in Middle French. When, however, the word appears again in the phrase *besoigne arrestee* Charny seems to be using a more specific term, one that overlaps with the common meaning of battle or *bataille:* a pitched, set, or stationary conflict between two sides who have to some degree sought out a decision and are intent on fighting it out.[25] In such a situation, the meaning and possibility of surrendering, always a course of action that, however common, might adversely affect one's reputation for honor, became even trickier. At Morlaix in 1342, Charny himself surrendered in a fight that might be called a *besoigne arrestee.* It is interesting to see him apparently rejecting surrender as a possibility in a set battle some time before he rejected the possibility for himself at Poitiers.

Another example of Charny discussing terminology and its relationship to evaluating honorable behavior can be seen in question W25, which states that there are two kinds of war,

> *(W25)... One kind is* guerre guerriable, *which takes place as a dispute from one frontier to another in disdain of one lord for another, and which often is able to move from one frontier to another in a variety of ways. The other kind of war is the desire to conquer a country, which one claims as lord but another lord holds.*

Guerre guerriable is difficult to translate in a short phrase, especially since Charny's two-war categorization differs from the four-war categorization reconstructed by Maurice Keen from later (mostly fifteenth-century) legal texts. Keen, however, cites a debate in the Parlement of Paris in 1433 which shows that it was relevant and necessary in a ransom case to contrast *guerre guerriable,* "a war fought under the feudal *droit de guerre,*" with *guerre mortelle,* sometimes called Roman war, a war against enemies such as the Saracens, who did not deserve the privilege of ransom, but were to be enslaved or killed.[26] Charny strongly contrasts his two types of war, if not in the same way: one is a war of conquest, the other is presumably more limited:

> *(W25) And this kind of war of conquest ought not to be waged. Some say war is more suitable in the manner of* guerre guerriable. *And so I ask how a war of conquest ought to be conducted.*

Charny's ambiguity strikes again. Is he upholding civilized limits on war against a more brutal standard being established by English efforts in the Hundred Years War? Or does he wish to discuss the differences between the two wars to remind people that the current conflict is much more uncompromising than what they have been used to in their private, regional wars? Although Charny's phrasing seems to evoke a positive view of *guerre guerriable,* it was not just the English in the early war years who applied the standards of all-out war to the conflict. The red Oriflamme, which was taken by the English to signal that the French would give no quarter, had flown at Crécy, and Charny himself would carry it at Poitiers, where again it was seen as the no-quarter banner.[27] In the end we cannot be sure either of Charny's stance, nor how his perhaps off-the-cuff definitions of *guerre guerriable* and the kind of war rooted in "the desire to conquer a country," relate to other, later categorizations of kinds of war.

The war of conquest makes another appearance in question W27, where a quite complex situation is sketched out. A lord who claims a country and is waging a war of conquest against its current lord, is besieging a city. Eventually the city can't hold out any longer and its current lord mounts a relief expedition. Yet when he comes to the city he finds that the besieger's army is so fortified that it can't be attacked. The current lord of the country then asks the lord besieging the city to fight in the open field, which someone with ambitions to conquer the country should be willing to dare. In the classic logic of deeds of arms, the current lord "makes it known to [the besieger] that when he calls himself lord of the country which is not his, that he will not be able to refuse him if he wishes to conquer it." The besieger refuses the challenge; he says that once the city falls he will be willing to fight. Charny asks:

> *(W27) So it should be decided which is more honorable: either to refuse battle against him who holds the country of which he calls himself lord and conqueror and remain before the city until he has taken it, or to go from it and fight... especially when he has enough men-at-arms and foot to fight if he wishes?*

Although this is a question that might be debated by lawyers, Charny does not present this as something to be submitted to the law of arms. The case is presented as a matter of honor. As Contamine noticed, this is an exact description of a confrontation between King Jean's father Philip and Edward III at Calais.[28] Following Crécy, Edward had taken his victorious force to Calais, a convenient port very close to England, and besieged it for a year. Eventually Philip was able to assemble a good force to attempt a relief, but as in the question, Edward was well ensconced in walled fortifications of his own and was unwilling to give up his advantage. Philip could not force him to do so, and Calais fell to the English.

I have no doubt that the entire point of this question was to stigmatize Edward and his cause as basically outside the usual standards of honor. Question W27 is therefore a unique attempt by Charny to use the war questions to praise the cause of his own king. The success of this effort depends in large part on agreement in the audience about appropriate standards of behavior, even in the most serious of wars, a consensus that may or may not have existed before Charny started working on them. This may seem to be the most direct and practical application of Charny's format for discussion of the laws of arms, but we cannot exclude the possibility that other questions and situations found in them were more topical and immediately relevant than we can know today.

Certainly we see in questions W17 and W18 Charny referring to a specialized terminology to promote his views on the moral foundations of chivalry. In these questions Charny claims to be ignorant of how one defines men who are *preux* and those who are *vaillans*. He asks in W17 "what [those who are *preux* or called *preudoms*] should necessarily have done before they bear this... honorable name;" in W18 he asked for a definition of valiant men, and whether "they are worth more than those who are *preux*, or less?" We may be seeing here a pose on Charny's part, because when he wrote the *Book of Chivalry*, he had very well developed notions of what each term meant and what kind of man was worthy of those designations. Briefly, and following Elspeth Kennedy's translation of the *Book of Chivalry*, Charny used the adjective *preux* and the noun *preudom* to mean "worthy" (among other things) and "men of worth." Men of worth combined several key virtues discussed in the *Book of Chivalry*. They were of course courageous and skilled in arms, but also generous, devout, and intelligent. They were leaders and counselors when such were needed. They combined physical toughness with consistent effort and a demonstrated desire from youth to learn all aspects of the life of arms. They were truly wise and lacking in vices. The *vaillans* were a step above that; in Kennedy's translation, they were men of "high merit," or "supreme worth." They had both prowess and wisdom, indeed the best kind of intelligence, and the best type of worth, the best kind of true and loyal prowess. Finally men of supreme worth never forgot that their virtues and accomplishments came from the grace of God; they knew that anyone who felt that his blessings came from his own personal merit would soon see those blessings crumble away to nothing. Since we do not know whether the *Questions* or the *Book of Chivalry* was written first, we can only speculate whether Charny had already made up his mind about the characteristics of the very best men-at-arms, and the words that should be used to describe them, or whether he was still working on these ideas when he wrote down these two queries. These questions, however, show a close connection between this project and the more extensive literary works produced by Charny. Charny's nuts and bolts discussions of the rights of individual men-at-arms were not divorced in his mind from discussions of what good men-at-arms should know about honorable behavior—nor, for that matter, military science.

We are not yet finished with the investigation of honor. There remain a number of miscellaneous didactic questions, none of which are presented as cases to be decided by the law of arms, but all of which discuss what is more suitable or more honorable behavior. Some of these we have seen before. I have grouped the questions into four categories. The first group is made up of only three questions which are uniquely concerned with the practical management of an army. One of these, W32, concerns the guards of the camp who stayed in place as ordered instead of reacting when their camp was attacked elsewhere on its perimeter in the middle of the night. The apparently passive behavior of the guardsmen is implicitly criticized, but it is not a matter of law: "Which should be more praised to remain in their ordained place... or to have come to the rescue the army... what do you think is better and more honorable?" A more unusual case is presented by W19, which compares the accomplishments of three followers of the same captain: one acting as a bodyguard, another as the captain's banner bearer, and the third who has not taken part in the same battle at all, but is a castellan of one of the captain's strong points. The worthy deeds of the first two are very briefly described, but Charny waxes eloquent and writes at length about how the castellan has overcome tremendous difficulties to save his lord's castle:

> *(W19) ...by the body, the holy effort and the difficult work of the castellan, the castle is not taken; rather he has held and defended it courageously so that the siege, which lasted so long, is lifted. And those in the castle praise the castellan, while his enemies say many good things about him. So the castellan renders the castle loyally to his lord, as a good man ought to do. Which of these would you prefer to resemble, as the one who had done the best of the three?*[29]

The praise of the castellan is so fulsome that only the dullest could miss Charny's favoritism. Why so? Is it perhaps because Charny himself was a castellan holding a difficult position in 1346, when others were doing more obvious service to their king at Crécy? It is interesting that the third and most practical question about army management is also about the proper preparation and supplying of a garrison by a commander who is charged to hold the castle for a year (W34).

The second category of miscellaneous questions comprise four or five obvious questions which both refer to honorable behavior and are based on ideas found in Charny's *Book of Chivalry*; in other words, questions whose answers can be reasonably guessed at. Questions of this sort clearly create openings for Charny to instruct his audience. Can we doubt what he would say (W92) about "which makes more sense in making war, knowing how to flee or how to pursue?" (It is interesting to speculate whether any members of the order might disagree, and if so why.) Charny wrote at some length in the *Book of Chivalry* about the superiority of deeds of arms of war to those of peace; that and the stated aims of the order tell us how Charny would have answered W91. Likely Charny also used question W93 to discuss courage and obligation, or perhaps the fact that not all who are called knights actually perform the role; but whether it was worse to leave a battlefield without striking a blow than to surrender without striking a blow I cannot say. Three further questions spring from Charny's belief that good men-at-arms should always be looking for opportunities to do more; resting on one's laurels was no part of his worldview. Thus it would be better (W36) for the captain who had lost a castle to know how to regain it, than for his enemy to be satisfied that he had taken and held it. One of the most entertaining questions in the entire list (W86) probably resolves itself by similar logic. No matter how well a group of men-at-arms had been entertained by worthy ladies in a neutral city, the anticipation by their enemies of a future revel with other worthy ladies in the same city should be more inspiring than the first group's memories.

A last category of didactic questions constitutes the truly miscellaneous ones, those whose context or logic is so obscure that finding a solution seems hopeless (W88), or those which present alternatives that are so well balanced that they seem to be exercises meant to inspire vigorous debate. Some have a look of classic topics that might have been kicked around for centuries before Charny included them in his list. "Which do you prefer: intelligence or prowess [*ou sens ou prouuesce*]?" may well have been argued since the days of the *Song of Roland* or even before:

> *Roland said: "Why are you angry with me?"*
> *The other [Oliver] replies: "Comrade, you brought this upon yourself,*
> *For heroism [vasselage] tempered with common sense [sens] is a far cry from madness;*
> *Reasonableness is to be preferred to recklessness.*
> *Frenchmen have died because of your senselessness.*
> *We shall never again be of service Charles.*
> *If you had believed me, my Lord would have come,*
> *We would have fought or won this*[30] *battle, King Marsile would be captured or slain.*
> *I have come to rue your prowess [proëcce], Roland!"*[31]

Others may have become classics afterwards. Question 85 is extraordinarily interesting: a hundred mounted men-at-arms bearing swords but wearing no spurs face off against another hundred who have spurs but no swords. In which group would you prefer to be? The very existence of the question assumes that Charny's contemporaries could see this as an interesting and even fight, and it gives us an unexpected insight into how vital control of a warhorse was for the practical warrior. This scenario's fascination is only increased by the fact that it is the one of Charny's questions we know from another source. About 140 years later, a hermit in the chivalric novel *Tirant lo Blanc* posed three questions to some young knights. The first is "Which would you rather be: strong but not skillful, or skillful but not strong?" about which "There were many opinions among the knights." Then the hermit asked which they would prefer:

> *To enter battle with sword but no spurs, or with spurs but no sword, for I can tell you I have witnessed such combats. I even saw one, fought before the Duke of Milan, in which two knights chose to joust in equal armor, but one was on horseback with only a sword, while the other was on foot with a lance and dagger. Who do you think had the advantage?*[32]

It certainly seems possible that both Charny and the authors of *Tirant lo Blanc* were drawing on a chivalric culture of debate in these passages.

Endnotes

1. For a classic anthropological treatment see J.G. Péristiany, ed., *Honour and Shame: the Values of Mediterranean Society* (Chicago: University of Chicago Press, 1966).
2. Kaeuper and Kennedy, 183.
3. Kaeuper and Kennedy, 87.
4. Kaeuper and Kennedy, 89.
5. Kaeuper and Kennedy, 113–115.
6. Kaeuper and Kennedy, 119.
7. Kaeuper and Kennedy, 109.
8. Kaeuper and Kennedy, 101–3.
9. Kaeuper and Kennedy, 101.
10. Kaeuper and Kennedy, 183.
11. Kaeuper and Kennedy, 87, 89, 115.

12. Kaeuper and Kennedy, 177–9. See also p. 179. This is one of the few places where Charny discusses the underside of waging war that so many non-warriors complained about during the Hundred Years War.
13. Kaeuper and Kennedy, 129.
14. Keen, *Laws of War,* 19–22.
15. Muhlberger, *Deeds of Arms* discusses this at length.
16. Kaeuper and Kennedy, 179.
17. Charny's whole treatise leans towards identifying men of a certain rank with worthy warriors, but he cannot help admitting that some who claim they "would never commit such wicked deeds... have them done by their own men." Ibid.
18. Boulton, 181.
19. Kaeuper and Kennedy, 133.
20. Kaeuper and Kennedy, 133.
21. The *Book of Chivalry,* or at least the first half of it, is a discussion of various kinds of wars that a man arms can participate in, and how they contribute to his reputation.
22. Keen, *Origins of the English Gentleman: Heraldry, Chivalry and Gentility in Medieval England, c.1300–c.1500* (Stroud, Gloucestershire: Tempus, 2002), 50.
23. Froissart 5:456–7.
24. See the discussion of bodyguards' dilemmas re: honor below at n. 210.
25. Thus the rather small Combat of the Thirty against Thirty was appropriately called a *bataille* by the anonymous Breton poet.
26. Keen *Laws of War,* 104–6,108–9:1. War to the death = *guerre mortelle* = Roman war. 2. Public war = open war = *bellum hostile.* 3. Feudal war = covered war (*guerre couverte*) = *guerre guerriable.* 4. Truce.
27. Keen, *Laws of War,* 105.
28. Contamine, *Guerre,* 190.
29. On the labor of the worthy man-at-arms, see Kaeuper, *Holy Warriors,* 135–44.
30. Editor inserts "(?)".
31. Gerard J. Brault, ed., *The Song of Roland: An Analytical Edition.* 2 vols. (University Park, Pa.: Pennsylvania State University Press, 1978) 2:107.
32. Martorell and Galba, 102.

7 OMISSIONS AND CONCLUSIONS

What Charny Left Out

I take what Charny has to say on the subjects of honor, military science, and chivalric lore to be valuable indicators of what we might call chivalric culture in the first half of the fourteenth century. As with the purely legal matters discussed in the previous chapter, these cases concern solely men-at-arms. In the *Book of Chivalry* Charny has a bit to say about the need for virtuous behavior towards noncombatants; he briefly adjures men-at-arms not to oppress the weak whether men, women or children, and says more about the need of rulers, men-at-arms writ large, to keep in mind their role as protectors, champions and good governors of all the rest.[1] There is no equivalent passage in the *Questions on War*. In the *Book of Chivalry* Charny is quite eloquent on the importance of love both to the lady who loves a worthy man and to the man-at-arms who is inspired by and loves her, yet the ladies of the neutral city who give praise and good company to warriors in W86 are the only women of any sort to appear in the *Questions*, and the only noncombatants. There is no hint of a clerical presence, or any thought expressed that clerical standards might apply to the issues raised by Charny.[2] A modern observer might call the *Questions* a secular document; I suspect that—despite a few digressions into theoretical territory—Charny would have characterized them as "practical, meant for practical men."

Yet not even all subjects of interest to soldiers and their masters are included. Unlike Giovanni da Legnano (and following him, Bouvet), Charny's *Questions* have nothing to say on reprisals and letters of marque, and next to nothing on duels. One can perhaps attribute this to the different political environments that Charny and Legnano wrote in. Legnano wrote in Italy where wars were often between cities with small territories and jurisdictions, but near-sovereign pretentions. The use of reprisals was easy and practical, and the complexities of sorting out questions of jurisdiction something many warriors—and lawyers—would have needed to be aware of. In a discussion in France among French *chevaliers,* one that took place in the presence of the king, a debate of this sort would be less relevant, and maybe even offensive to the sovereign claims of the Prince of the Order.

A similar explanation accounts for the near-absence of duels from the *Questions* (but see W65, 84). Duels, like Beaumanoir's *guerre,* were a noble privilege, or had been, or were visualized as such by the military aristocracy, and in the form of judicial combats had been a routine part of judicial practice in the past.[3] In fourteenth-century France, however, judicial combats had fallen in disfavor, at least in the eyes of the royal legal establishment. King Jean's ancestor Philip IV had legislated in such a way as to restrict them severely, and they hardly ever were allowed to take place. Again, this was a subject that may not have been diplomatic to raise before a king who was doing his best to discipline or at least unify his ranking warriors around the cause of effective royal authority. [4]

Another subject that might have appeared in Charny's questions, one that hardly wanders very far from law of arms, is "arms" in the heraldic sense. Keen's *Laws of War* mentions a fourteenth-century case where a dispute over armorial bearings came before courts made up of ranking men-at-arms.[5] The right to wear a certain set of arms was a treasured family inheritance tied closely to one's status as a respectable warrior; arms were not borne by civilians or by corporations as they were later, and are in some places still today. As something pertaining to warrior status and warrior culture, the rights and wrongs of a given case naturally were judged by others of the same status, or by higher military authorities. In England such cases sometimes progressed to the Court of Chivalry, presided over by the Constable and Earl Marshal. In a few cases we have a fair amount of surviving documentation including testimony by appropriate witnesses, who are almost entirely knights and squires. The English case of Scrope v. Grosvenor is the best known. Adjudicated in the 1380s, it generated an elaborate process, which lasted for years; the dispute finally had to be settled by the king himself. The surviving testimony is extensive and makes clear that the plaintiffs and defendants and their peers took heraldic conflicts extremely seriously, and felt their honor intimately entwined and identified with the respect shown to their chosen or inherited arms.[6] There is plenty of evidence that this attitude towards heraldry existed in many parts of Europe, and certainly in France, so Charny's indifference to discussing cases based on heraldry is curious.

There is another area ignored by Charny where the indifference is also hard to account for and that is the complete lack of interest in the complex rules and conventions that governed relations between the besieging army and those inside the stronghold or walled city under attack. Modern scholars usually consider these protocols or customs as part of the "laws of war," reflecting a phrase that was certainly used in connection with sieges during the fifteenth century.[7] The existence of such a framework of custom was much older. Jim Bradbury has argued that the conventions and laws of siege warfare were of ancient origin and predated both Christianity and Islam.[8] At the very least, he says that "the making of surrender terms of the kind of terms enforced" were much the same from the fall of the Roman Empire to the Reformation.[9] It is a commonplace of military history and history of war crimes to regard sieges as a special case of warfare which "have always been treated as total war."[10]

It seems somewhat curious to me that Charny's survey of legal problems inherent in war has nothing whatever about two aspects of behavior at sieges. The first of these was the set of customs governing surrender. Sieges were far more important and common in the Middle Ages than set battles; the winner of a siege secured territory in a way that the winner of the rare major battle could only envy. Sieges were often very hard fought, and emotions ran high. Sometimes the civilian population of the town would take a very active part in defending its walls, knowing that keeping them intact was their only hope of safety, whatever other issues may have been at stake. Projectiles of various sorts were shot in both directions, to the dismay and anger of the living targets. Usually both sides suffered from illness and hunger. Sieges were serious business and those who mounted them quite logically took a ruthless attitude to the people they wished to conquer. They did their best to terrorize garrisons and civilian populations into a quick surrender by threatening unlimited violence if the place was taken. In particular, everyone knew that once the besieger had brought up his siege engines (later, artillery), it was too late to negotiate terms; a town or strong point could expect no mercy—though sometimes it was granted anyway.

Another set of customs regulated the obligations of garrison commanders and even civil populations to an absent overlord. While the besieging captain was hotly urging quick surrender or else, the lord of the stronghold was observing those to whom he had entrusted the defense. In his eyes, and not in his alone, a too-quick surrender was treason, the result of a payoff. For the security of both the hired garrison commander and his lord, it became common during the Hundred Years War to specify precisely under which conditions a strongpoint could be surrendered.

Why did Charny not discuss the legal problems that might surround these important military matters?[11] From the point of view of noncombatant observers, one of the worst aspects of war was the rape, plunder, and slaughter of people who had very little say in whether a town or castle was defended or surrendered. Many modern observers would think that this is precisely the kind of thing that deserved to be regulated. Sometimes medieval observers lamented the destruction of towns and their inhabitants as the most horrible feature of war. Concerning the famous sack of Limoges, perpetrated by Edward Prince of Wales in 1370 in revenge for the town throwing off his lordship and returning to French allegiance, the chronicler Froissart said:

> *There was not that day in the city of Limoges any heart so hardened, or that had any sense of religion, who did not deeply bewail the unfortunate events passing before their eyes; for upwards of three thousand men, women and children were put to death that day. God have mercy on their souls! for they were veritable martyrs.*

But this is very deceptive, as is Froissart's statement earlier on:

> *I know not why the poor were not spared, who could not have had any part in this treason; but they suffered for it, and indeed more than those who had been the leaders of the treachery.*

He knew why:

> *You would then [when the English army broke through into the town] have seen pillagers, active to do mischief, running through the town, slaying men, women, and children,* ***according to their orders****. It was a most melancholy business; for all ranks, ages and sexes cast themselves on their knees before the prince, begging for mercy;* ***but he was so inflamed with passion and revenge that he listened to none****, but all were put to the sword...*[12]

Froissart knew that such "atrocities," a word that perhaps inaccurately implies that it was a matter of armies getting out of control, were pretty common and could be considered a legitimate tactic of war. It was a widespread practice to turn over a town taken by storm to the army for three days, and monarchs justified this harshness as a punishment for obduracy.[13]

By this time the reader understands that whatever we think the law of arms should have covered, Charny clearly thought that the relationship between warriors and non-warriors was not part of it. But this explanation is quite insufficient for ignoring the law of sieges, since sieges also created relationships between men-at-arms, both those on the same side and those opposed to each other. For instance, who was a legitimate target of the "punishment"—for punishment it was seen to be—when the town was taken? Let us return to the sack of Limoges, to an incident which opened Maurice Keen's *Laws of War* more than forty years ago. There is a passage in Froissart's account where three French men-at-arms, expecting death, decide to "sell [their] lives dearly":

> *These three Frenchmen did many valorous deeds of arms, as all allowed, and ill did it betide those who approached too near. The prince, coming that way in his carriage, looked on the combat with great pleasure, and enjoyed it so much that his heart was softened and his anger appeased. After the combat had lasted a considerable time, the Frenchmen, with one accord, viewing their swords, said, "My lords, we are yours: you have vanquished us: therefore act according to the law of arms." "By God," replied the duke of Lancaster, "Sir John, we do not intend otherwise, and we accept you for our prisoners."*[14]

For Keen, this was one episode among several that piqued his curiosity about the meaning of the term "law of arms." As he said, "the knights were clearly appealing to some sort of general code of military conduct, which they believed the combatants on either side in any war should feel bound to honor," in this case by acknowledging their claim to "a right to quarter."[15] But Keen never actually dealt with this kind of case. If he had, it would have posed a pretty puzzle. When it came to lawful behavior of sieges, none of the treatise writers had much if anything to say about the "law" (which we know was referred to on occasion at least in the fifteenth century) that regulated or mollified effects of warfare on urban populations or defeated garrisons. This is even the case in Honoré Bouvet's *Tree of Battles*, which contains several disapproving remarks about how men-at-arms break laws when convenient.

It is my conclusion that the law of sieges clearly existed in customary form, but was not ever codified because what happened at sieges was the dirty secret of the military profession. What happened at sieges, according to a sixteenth-century soldier, when the same customs were used, "makes the generous base, and great men do those things they blush to think on."[16] Rape, torture, and murder could not be justified by argument in a Christian court, so the less said the better about the cruelty that benefited both successful commanders and their men. The traditional explanation, still found in modern scholarship, is that this mistreatment of defeated civilians was "misconduct," or exceptional behavior, not a central part of the waging of war in pre-modern times. We do not see Charny making such an argument in regard to sieges, but it is worth remembering how he explained all misdeeds of war as being the behavior of men-at-arms who were not really men-at-arms, without getting into details or considering any practical measures beyond the general idea that a commander should control his men.[17] Charny was likely not indifferent about what happened to the unarmed population during war. Dealing with that problem, however, was not his priority. His key goal in his dealings with King Jean and with the Order of the Star was to make the chivalry of France braver and more effective, not kinder. Kindness was a rare commodity in the ever-growing war whose early years provided the backdrop of his military career.

Conclusion: The Law of Arms for Men-at-Arms

Charny's *Questions* were an attempt to codify something that had been very vague in the past, and in which some ways continued to be vague. Maurice Keen's *Laws of War*, still the essential survey of the subject, traced out the long evolution of military law during the period of the Hundred Years War, and showed how various sources and ideas contributed to that evolution. Charny's *Questions*, which Keen noted only in passing, deserves to be recognized as one of the earliest attempts at systematizing such law. The *Questions* perhaps can be regarded as the fruit of one regional tradition as remembered by knights before the need generated by a vast series of international wars transformed the field and made it a matter of general and ongoing interest to legal professionals. The existence of the *Questions* is an indication that some men of rank—at the very least Charny himself—were recognizing the need for a formal law of arms and the involvement of warriors in establishing its principles. One of the most interesting aspects of the *Questions* is the way it went beyond the ordinances issued by kings and commanders to keep order in specific armies during specific campaigns to reach for general principles.

On the other hand, the *Questions* address only a limited set of concerns, the rights and privileges of men-at-arms. Since the audience for Charny's proposed discussion was entirely composed of men-at-arms—fully-equipped and trained warriors—and prominent ones at that, it makes sense that their discussion would be biased in that direction. The subject matter, however, so thoroughly excludes consideration of the effects of *guerre*—or *armes* —on women, clergy, other non-combatants and even commoner members of armies that one can hardly avoid the conclusion that Charny's audience believed that men-at-arms like themselves had the deciding authority in determining how things should work, that the law of arms was a law of, by and for men-at-arms. Perhaps Charny himself felt that way, or perhaps he felt the need to appeal to such a proud class-conscious attitude if he was going to influence the leading French *chevaliers* in the direction he wished them to go; a direction, one might say, of greater professionalism.

The self-regarding nature of the *Questions,* and the limits of its imagination of war can be seen by comparing Charny's corpus to any of a number of army ordinances of the late Middle Ages, such as the English and French ones preserved in the *Black Book of the Admiralty*. Reading these and other ordinances dispels immediately any notion that ranking warriors of the period were selfishly impractical, at least that they were selfishly impractical all the time. Such ordinances, which have different emphases depending on their particular purposes are sensible guides to accomplishing those purposes: regulating camp behavior, assembling and organizing armies, even planning battles and campaigns. These ordinances were all composed and implemented by men just like Charny.

If that prominent politician and general focused his *Questions* on the rights and privileges and duties of men-at-arms, let us assume that he had good reason. Charny believed, as did his king, that noble warriors were an essential element in society—an order—and that the health of the sorely-abused kingdom of France required them to remember and practice their way of life, the life of arms, and to revitalize the order of chivalry by rededicating themselves to it. One of the necessary steps to this revitalization was to be the redefinition of the law of arms. Charny's *Questions,* in laying the groundwork for that redefinition, give us a unique window on the common values that held the community of men-at-arms together. The very limitations of the *Questions,* and our effortful attempts to understand those values, make the *Questions* a resource that should be studied by everyone interested in the era of the Hundred Years War.

Endnotes

1. Kaeuper and Kennedy, 140–7.
2. The active debate between clerical and lay authors on questions of war and chivalry has recently been discussed at length by Kaeuper in *Holy Warriors* and *Chivalry and violence in medieval Europe* (Oxford: Oxford University Press, 1999).
3. The relationship between judicial combats and other forms of noble "deeds of arms" is explored in Muhlberger, *Deeds of Arms*, 47–75.

4. W65 describes a quarrel that leads to a fight resulting in the loser being captured. It is worth noting that this situation can arise only in a special environment, "in a country where one is allowed to take others as prisoners."
5. 34.
6. Keen, *Origins of the English Gentleman*, 25–70 for a discussion of the Court of Chivalry and its role not just in heraldic cases but also in others concerning the law of arms as Charny would have recognized it. The Scrope-Grosvenor case is documented in *De controversia in curia militari inter Ricardum Le Scrope et Robertum Grosvenor milites rege Ricardo Secundo, MCCCLXXXV-MCCCXC e recordis in turre Londinensi asservatis.* (London: Printed by Samuel Bentley, 1832).
7. Jim Bradbury, *The Medieval Siege* (Woodbridge: Boydell Press, 1992) 308, 311–2 and n. 38: "bellorum jura."
8. Bradbury, 296.
9. Bradbury, 333.
10. Geoffrey Parker, "Early Modern Europe," in Michael Howard, George J. Andreopoulos, and Mark R. Shulman. *The Laws of War: Constraints on Warfare in the Western World* (New Haven: Yale University Press, 1994), 45.
11. Exception: W34 touches on the obligations of a castellan to the castle's lord.
12. Froissart 8:43; Johnes, 1:453–4.
13. Bradbury, 318, 323.
14. Froissart, 8:43; Johnes, 1:454.
15. Keen, *Laws of War*, 1.
16. Geoffrey Parker, *Success is never final: empire, war, and faith in early modern Europe* (N.Y.: Basic Books, 2002), 155.
17. Kaeuper and Kennedy, Adam Roberts, "Land Warfare: from Hague to Nuremberg," in Corfis and Wolfe, *The Medieval City Under Siege*, reference to lack of specific laws of war until *1977*.

INTRODUCTION TO THE TRANSLATIONS

This appendix includes two texts: my full translation of Charny's *Questions Concerning the Joust, Tournaments, and War* and Francis Grose's translation of Richard II's military ordinance issued at Durham in 1385.

The translation of Charny's *Questions* is my own. It is based on the edition of Michael Anthony Taylor, who edited the *Questions* as part of his doctoral dissertation at the University of North Carolina, Chapel Hill, in 1977. I have also included material from Jean Rossbach's edition, Brussels, 1961–2. That material consists of an additional question found only in the margin of the Madrid manuscript, which I have designated W80A, and a marginal answer to question 44 (85) in the same manuscript. Neither editor felt that these items were Charny's work, but I thought that they would interest the reader anyway.

I translated some relevant questions in my *Jousts and Tournaments* in 2002. The revised versions here are to be preferred.

The Ordinance of Richard II can be found in the *Black Book of the Admiralty* 1:453–8, and this translation comes from Francis Grose, *Military antiquities respecting a history of the English army, from the Conquest to the present time*, 2 vols. (London: 1801) 2:64–9. It is here as an example of how ranking men-at-arms thought about armies and waging war when they were not entirely concerned with their own rights and privileges. It is an English document but has the advantage of coming from only a generation later than Charny's time, and being the product of a French-speaking military establishment shaped by the Hundred Years War.

QUESTIONS CONCERNING THE JOUST, TOURNAMENTS, AND WAR

I: Questions on the Joust

These are the questions concerning the joust which I, Geoffroy de Charny, pose to the high and mighty prince of the Knights of Our Lady of the Noble House to be judged by you and the knights of our noble company.

1. First I ask: An *emprise* for jousting is announced for a certain place on a certain day to deliver all knights of three lances and not more, and nothing else is announced except the prize. So it happens that one knight knocks another to the ground and out of the saddle with a stroke of the lance. Will he who knocks the other to the ground win the other's horse? What do you say in this case, will it not be judged by the law of arms?
2. Charny asks: If it happened that in this celebration one knight knocked another to the ground with a stroke of the lance, his saddle being between his legs and the whole thing off the horse, will he who knocked the other down win the horse? What do you say in this case, will it not be judged by the laws of arms?
3. Charny asks: Knights are jousting without a formal announcement, and one knight knocks another down and out of the saddle with a stroke of the lance. Will he who knocked the other down win the horse? What do you say?
4. Charny asks: An *emprise* for squires takes place with jousting in the same manner as in the announcement above, and in no other way. One squire knocks another to the ground and out of the saddle. Will he win the horse? What do you say?
5. Charny asks: In the *emprise* it is said that anyone who kills a horse with a stroke of a lance will pay for it. So it happens that in jousting one strikes the other's horse with his lance well advanced; but their horses collide so hard that both of them fall to the ground. Will he who struck the horse with the lance pay for it or not? What do you say?
6. Charny asks: Knights and squires joust in an *emprise*, with the announced rules as above. One knight knocks a squire out of the saddle, or a squire does the same to a knight. Will he win the horse? What do you say?
7. Charny asks: An *emprise* is arranged for jousting by either knights or squires, with the announced rules as above. So it happens that one of the home team jousts in this way with one of the visitors, and because he was running out of bounds, the visitor throws his lance and the thrown lance strikes its butt end on the ground. And before the front end falls down it pierces the other's horse and kills it. Does the visitor give recompense for the horse? What do you say?

8. Charny asks: A banneret sends out from his entourage some knights to go out with him in the fields to joust with those who have set the *emprise*; those knights agree with him and sally forth on their own horses which are with them. If there are two or three of them whose horses are dead and injured in the joust from blows or falls, will the banneret be obliged to compensate them? What do you say?
9. Charny asks: There is an *emprise* as above. It happens that one of the visitors jousts with one of the home team; and the home jouster strikes the visitor's horse on the head or some other part, and it was the visitor's first course. So he does not wish at all to get down before he has run the two lances which he has yet to run; and when he has run them he sends the horse to the defender, and demands that he compensate him. Will he compensate him? What do you say?
10. Charny asks: There is an *emprise* as above. A horse is struck by a lance and the one who is riding it dismounts right away and sends it to his inn. The next day he sends it to the inn of the man who struck it. Will he pay him compensation? What do you say?
11. Charny asks: Two knights joust in the contest described above and at the striking of the lances both come out of the saddle. Will each take the horse of his companion, or each keep his own? What do you say?
12. Charny asks: A squire, completely armed for jousting, enters an *emprise* for knights and jousts; and a knight of the *emprise* knocks him out of the saddle with the stroke of the lance. Will the knight win the horse, for each believed that he was a knight until he was down, but he did not wear any golden accoutrements. How will it be judged according to the law of arms?
13. Charny asks: A knight, armed as a knight, enters and jousts in an *emprise* for squires; and a squire in the *emprise* knocks him out of the saddle with a stroke of the lance. Will the squire win the horse? What do you say? What do others think?
14. Charny asks: A knight of the *emprise* strikes with his spurs, and two of the visiting knights, each one aiming with his lance, come against him. And the home knight hits the first of the two with his lance and knocks him out of the saddle, and the second strikes the home knight. And with the same blow, the visiting knight knocks himself out of the saddle; and at the time of the blow the home knight did not have a lance. Will the home knight win the two horses from the visitors? What do you say?
15. Charny asks: A knight of the *emprise* strikes with his spurs, aiming with his lance, and another visiting knight striking with his spurs comes against him at the same time. So it happens that one of the two also as he is coming to strike him puts his lance into the ground, and by this blow knocks himself out of the saddle and onto the ground. Will the other win his horse? What do you say, for the one has not struck the other?
16. Charny asks: A knight of the *emprise* described above strikes his spurs and in his first course is wounded and disarms himself; and another puts on his harness and mounts his horse to joust in the place of him who was wounded with the agreement of the wounded man, even though he was not at all part of the *emprise*, but is only to aid those who had established the *emprise*. So he jousts so well that none of the home team in the judgment of all comes even close to him. Who will have the prize, he who jousted so well, or his master for whom he jousted, or whoever has jousted best among those holding the *emprise* next to him? What do you say?

17. Charny asks: This aforesaid knight who has jousted so well for his master, that same day struck a horse with his lance, which horse was sent to him because he should pay recompense for it. Will he pay recompense, or his master? What do you say?
18. Charny asks: A knight who jousts at the above celebration has struck another with his lance and knocks him out of the saddle, except that with one of his hands he holds to the saddlebow, but otherwise he should be entirely out of the saddle; but no more of him remains on the saddle except his hand. Will he lose the horse and will the other win it? What do you say?
19. Charny asks: A knight or a squire has borrowed a horse for jousting from another companion and he jousts on; but nevertheless he happens to crash the horse into his companion's horse and equipment. When after three weeks or a month this companion returns the horse to the one from whom he borrowed it, that horse has not gained any value from the blows in any way that could be seen. And the companion who lent it refuses to take it, because of the blows, but wants to have the price of the horse. And so they are in contention. What do you say?
20. Charny asks: A knight knocks another to the ground with a blow of his lance, and his horse with him, and the horse is not able to get up if the knight does not get out of the saddle. So is he able to get out of the saddle without the permission of the one he jousted with? And if he dismounts without the permission of him whom he jousted with, and the horse gets up, is he who knocked it to the ground able to claim the horse by the law of arms for jousting? What do you say?

II: Questions on Tournaments

These are the questions concerning the tourney which I, Geoffroy de Charny, pose to the high and mighty prince of the Knights of Our Lady of the Noble House to be judged by you and the knights of your noble company.

1. First I ask: So a powerful man retains a banneret, or a banneret a knight, for a certain fee and for the season, and thus they are agreed; and afterwards they come to the city where the tourney has been proclaimed and arms displayed in the windows. So when the rich man or the banneret above comes without his banner and whole retinue, and another powerful man speaks to the banneret or knight above, suggesting he should be with him for a year; and the banneret, or the knight takes the offer. Then the powerful man who has retained him for a year goes to remove the banneret who is with the other and make him display his arms outside the windows with him. So is he able to do that by the law of arms for tourncys? What do you say?
2. Charny asks: So the powerful man who had retained that banneret for a season and who has lost him for the year, if it is thus said, speaks again to the banneret who has left him, saying that the other should be retained for life and gives him land for life, as long as they are in agreement. So then the powerful man goes to remove the banneret from the retinue of the powerful man who had retained him for the year, and take him back with him as before. The other powerful man says no. So can he do this by the law of arms for tourneys? What do you say?

3. Charny asks: If it was said that he was able to do this, and another powerful man gave to this banneret or bachelor a hereditary holding, and retained him, could the one who has retained him for life take him away by the law of arms for tourneys?
4. Charny asks: Are there the same contractual obligations for squires as is said above for knights by the law of arms for tourneys?
5. Charny asks: The judges come to take the oath of the knights in the accustomed manner and all give it except one bachelor who is not willing to swear. Will he remain to take part in the tourney or not by the law of arms for tourneys?
6. Charny asks: So the judge did not allow this knight to tourney, and this knight did not wish to arm himself, and the judge had "tie it up" cried and had the cords [or stakes] put in the fields, and people went out and the troops were made by the judges and they say "you are released" to them, and they clash. And there many are pulled to the ground and their horses are taken. And when the evening comes, those whose horses are lost ask for them back and say it was not a tourney at all. How will it be judged by the law of arms for tourneys?
7. Charny asks: The judges have "tie it up" cried and the stakes put in the fields. And when all the knights are in the field the judges organize the tourney and some troops. And those troops attack before they should have ordered the whole tourney into troops. And before they are able to order the tourney into the final troops there appear many more knights on the field; so the judges are not able to arrange any more of them into these troops. The other troops which have engaged lose and gain horses and are led to the stake. [Implied question: if the losers ask for their horses back and say that this was not a tourney at all, how will it be judged by the law of arms for tourneys?]
8. Charny asks: A knight sallies out all armed without any covering as above to tourney on a beautiful destrier. And when it comes time to ride out to the attack, this knight mounts a different horse. And an unarmed man mounts the horse he has got down from. And during the tourney, while he is struggling against that knight, that horse that the knight rode on and dismounted follows into the middle of the field, completely beyond the stakes. So some others catch the horse and take it to their boundary of the field and knock down the unarmed man who was on it and they say that they have won it. The knight says no. How should it be according to the law of arms for tourneys?
9. Charny asks: A knight tourneys with others as above and tourneys under mutually agreed rules; thus he is pulled to the ground and his horse, too. Those who have pulled him to the ground cut his girths and the breastplate of the saddle and the horse gets up. So they lead it to the stake and the knight remains on the ground with his saddle between his legs. Has the horse been won or lost by the knight? What will be said about it by the law of arms for tourneys?
10. Charny asks: A squire or two or three armed for the tourney find a knight outside of the mêlée. So they stop him and pull him down and take the horse off to the stake. When evening comes the knight demands his horse because there was no knight present at his loss. The squires say no. What should happen according to the law of arms for tourneys?
11. Charny asks: There is a tourney under mutually agreed rules and people are tourneying in it. When evening comes the stakes are taken up very late. But for a long time many knights remain on the field in a mêlée and they lose and win a number of horses on one side or the

other. And when the evening comes many ask for the return of their horses because they lost them when the stakes were taken up. What will be judged in this case according to the law of arms for tourneys?

12. Charny asks: If it was said, concerning any of the horses above demanded that evening, that some should be returned, if any others delay until the next day, should it be decided that those horses should be returned, as if they had asked in the evening?

13. Charny asks: A tourney is arranged with mutually agreed rules in a city and the stakes are placed and "tie it up" is cried and they sally forth. And at the point where they are outside, one or two bachelors arrive in the city who are not able to have their horses or harness that day. And because of this they do not remain, nor do they join a troop, nor attack. Will this be a tournament or not? What will you say in this case by the laws of arms for tourneys?

14. Charny asks: If they are between two cities and it happens just as it is described above, will these be tourneying or held to take part in preliminary fights (*encommensaille*)?

15. Charny asks: What is it that makes a tourney a tourney and not something else?

16. Charny asks: What is it that makes a preliminary fight (*encommensaille*) a preliminary fight and not something else?

17. Charny asks: What makes *toupineures* toupineures and not something else?

18. Charny asks: Which is to be more highly prized: The one who loses two horses or three in one day while attacking or defending quite openly, or one who keeps his horse very close the whole day and endures and bears well the pulls and blows and everything that comes his way? What do you say?

19. Charny asks: A banneret is going to a tourney and has his bachelors with him in his retinue; and he wishes to tourney with it during the week. And some of the bachelors with him go out to the preliminary combats and lose their horses, without the permission of their master and without their master being there. When evening comes they request the return of their horses, and their master says no. How will it be judged by the law of arms for tourneys?

20. Charny asks: A banneret comes during the week to tourney and does not wish to take part at his rank, but to take part under another as a bachelor. Also in the city are some companions who are retained by him for a year and these companions require him to give them their maintenance, both mounts and other things. Their master says no, because he does not wish to take that rank; and after this answer the two bachelors go to seek gain for a year with other masters. The first master says that they cannot do this. The bachelors say they can. How will it be judged by the law of arms for tourneys?

21. Charny asks: A knight and two squires are contracted for the tourney and for the year. The knight hastily comes into the city where he wishes to tourney, doesn't find his squires, and retains two others on the eve of the tourney. And when the morning comes the two squires who are retained for a year come before the hour of "tie it up!" and present themselves to him ready to serve him. The master refuses them for the day, for this day he has retained two others. Then the two squires retained for a year go to seek their gain with other masters for a year, and say they are able to do it. The first master says no. What will be judged in this case by the law of arms for tourneys?

III: Questions on War

These are the questions for war which I, Geoffroi de Charny, pose to the high and mighty prince of the Knights of Our Lady of the Noble House to be judged both you and the knights of your noble company.

1. First I ask: A lord has his whole army before a city and is besieging it, and that lord has many captains, and from other countries than his own. A man-at-arms who belongs to one of those captains leaves the army and goes to demand a stroke of the lance from one of the men-at-arms of the city, who sallies forth to deliver him. And having met him in combat, the companion from the city bears the one from the army out of the saddle with a stroke of the lance and takes the horse and leads it away into the city. And this was done in the morning. And that same day, when evening comes, another companion from the army, who belongs to a different captain than the first, goes to demand a stroke of the lance from those in the city. And the companion from the city who won the horse in the morning mounts the horse which he has won and goes out to deliver the companion from the army. So it happens that the companion from the army knocks the one from the city to the ground and takes the horse and leads it away to the army. Then he who lost the horse in the morning comes and demands it back as his own; and the one who won it in the evening says no. Many good arguments are put forward on one side or the other. How will it be judged by the law of arms?
2. Charny asks: Knights and squires of a lord have fees, expenses and harness from that lord. If a knight and a squire gain prisoners and plenty of other goods, those being the people mentioned above, what profit or what share will they have from being in the company of that lord, apart from death?
3. Charny asks: Knights joust with steel lances in an *emprise*. One knocks the other to the ground with a stroke of his lance. Will the one who has knocked the other to the ground and out of the saddle win the horse? How will it be judged by the law of arms?
4. Charny asks: Do squires have the same rights as knights in such a case?
5. Charny asks: If it was said that those mentioned above were able to lose or gain [horses], and a knight knocks a squire out of the saddle with a steel lance, or a squire a knight, what right will he have to the horse, or will it neither be lost nor gained?
6. Charny asks: A captain and lord of a country meets another one of the same sort in war; and they come to the point of combat. Which will be better: that the captain goes before his banner and his banner after him, or that the banner should be in front and the captain behind?
7. Charny asks: Two captains as described above fight each other. One is defeated but remains on the field so long that he sees and understands that he is unable to recover his fortunes or the day; and the battle has been very well fought. Which is the better thing for him to do: remain and take his chances, or leave so that he can recoup? And if he leaves, should he thereby lose his honor?
8. Charny asks: There are some people who are under orders to be bodyguards under the authority of a captain who has lost a battle. Which is the better thing to do: lead their master to safety, and in that case, either go with him, or send him outside of the melee alone, and tell him to save himself if he is able? There is a great risk that he will not be able to save

himself; and by returning into the battle they take the risk of death or capture. Since they have agreed to be men in his retinue, will they be blamed if they go with him? Which is better, to go or to stay?

9. Charny asks: Men-at-arms leave a city where they are in garrison and ride towards their enemies and ride by a city ten leagues from their own, and capture booty from the city and carry it away. The garrison of this city sallies out to reclaim their booty, and they fight with the outsiders. And it happens that those outside defeat those from the city and take possession of the field and take the booty they have won a good six leagues completely undisturbed, until they pass another city belonging to their enemies and involved in the same war; these two cities belong to the captain who is their enemy. And those in this city sally out and fight with those who are leading away the booty of the other city, and defeat them and take their gains and booty into the city. Those from the other city who lost the booty formerly hear that it has been regained in that city; so they come to ask for their booty, and those who regained it refuse. Many good arguments are put forward about it on one side or the other. How will it be judged by the law of arms?

10. Charny asks: A captain rides with well-ordered battalions before a good city of his enemies, and this captain has it announced that none should leave his formation. And while they are passing before this city many men-at-arms from the city show themselves outside the barriers. And some of the men-at-arms of the captain passing before this city strike their spurs against the men-at-arms of the city who have come out, and lose many of their horses and reassemble in their battalion before their captain. When they come back they ask for compensation for their horses, and the captain says no. Many good arguments are put forward about it on one side or the other. How will it be judged by the law of arms?

11. Charny asks: Men-at-arms meet each other in the field and fight each other and at the clash a man-at-arms knocks one of his enemies to the ground with the stroke of his lance, and out of the saddle, and the horse runs on. And the companion stops over him whom he has struck down both to take and protect him, and he does that. Another companion sees the horse, which the first does not appear to have taken, and he takes it and leads it away. When evening comes the one who struck down the man-at-arms asks for the horse as rightfully being his; the one who has the horse, refuses. Many good arguments are put forward about it on one side or the other. How will it be judged by the law of arms?

12. Charny asks: Two companions are at war with each other, so that one demands men-at-arms from his friends. In this company he has many horses borrowed from other people who are not in this war. So this companion rides out with all his men-at-arms and does great damage to his enemies. However those who have lost have recognized some of the borrowed horses. So it happens when the horses are returned to those by whom they were given, the companions whose horses have been lost find these horses and their owners and take them as in war. The owners reject this and demand their horses by right of arms, since the two groups should be at peace with each other. How will it be judged by the law of arms?

13. Charny asks: There are three types of combat in the field. One is called a *rencontre* (encounter). How is it called a rencontre and why, for some say that a rencontre takes place between a thousand men-at-arms or more on one side and the other? And if one party fights and defeats the other and takes possession of the field, if it is not called a *besoigne* (affair) nor a *bataille* (battle), how should it be designated, then?

14. Charny asks: Men-at-arms are in the field, and a thousand men or more fight; and one party defeats the other and takes possession of the field. And it is said that it was nothing but an affair, halted as it was by nightfall, and should not be called an encounter or a battle. How should it be designated?

15. Charny asks: When should a battle be called a battle and why that rather than something else?

16. Charny asks: Two captains are in the field to fight and there is a great number of men-at-arms on either side. And so one of the captains and his people are defeated. And the other captain who has overcome him has killed his people, taken a great number of the defeated and gained horses and plenty of other goods. And when the evening comes none consider this to be an encounter, an affair, or a battle. How can this be and what should it be called?

17. Charny asks: Because I do not know what kind of people are called *preux,* I ask what they should necessarily have done before they bear this name so that when they've done this they are able to have such an honorable name. For I believe that he who does more is worth more. But I ask what they should necessarily do at the minimum.

18. Charny asks: Because I have heard it said of another type of man which like the others I cannot define, who are called *vaillans* men: what kind of men are those and how, why, or in what way should they be considered as vaillans? Are they worth more than those who are preux or less? What is it proper for them to have done; and of what condition should they be to have this great name and none other?

19. Charny asks: There is a captain of a country who is fighting against his enemies; and there is one who has been ordered to be a bodyguard and under the authority of this lord. The one under the authority of this lord stays very close to this lord and keeps near him all day, and fights well and the captain defeats his enemies that day. There is another there who carries the captain's banner and carries it so well and so courageously and always harms the enemies of his lord, and bears arms that day as well as a good man ought to do in his position. There is another man with this lord who is castellan of a castle of the same lord, which castle is besieged by his enemies. And it is assaulted and attacked many times and for a long time, with many kinds of attack and engines by which the castle is very broken down, by arms and by other means; and some of the people in the castle are dead and many are wounded and they in the castle have suffered much distress. But nevertheless by the body, the holy effort and the difficult work of the castellan, the castle is not taken; rather, he has held and defended it courageously so that the siege, which had lasted so long, is lifted. And those in the castle praise the castellan, while his enemies say many good things about him. So the castellan renders the castle loyally to his lord, as a good man ought to do. Which of these would you prefer to resemble, as the one who had done best of the three?

20. Charny asks: Two captains are at war with one another and the one has many friends and the other does, too, and more of their lineages and others as well. And it happens that one has as many of his friends as he can get and goes against the other and damages the other greatly. And in the company of the captain who has been harmed by the other there is a powerful man who has more to lose than the other captain who has been attacked; and the powerful man has many of his friends and members of his lineage in the service of the

other captain who has been doing harm to the one who has been damaged, for they are more linked by lineage to the captain who has attacked him than they are to the other; but they are closer by lineage to the powerful man who has been harmed by the other. And the powerful man fears to lose his property; so he goes to his friends of his lineage who are with the other captain whom he has been opposed to; so he composes letters of defiance and sends them to that captain and defies him as a principal party along with him who has been harmed. And then he requires the members of his lineage who are with the other party to aid him against the captain against whom he wants to make war as a principal. And they respond that he is an ally, not a principal; for he came to war before as an ally, and now cannot make himself a principal party to the war. The powerful man says he can do this. What ought to be done by the law of arms, among all the good arguments that they know how to offer on either side, for by the custom of the country the chief can be chosen from among the helpers as much as from among the captains.

21. Charny asks: A knight or a squire strikes another in anger or by word; and the one who is struck finds himself the stronger and captures the one who struck him and leads him away and puts him in a strong, foul prison. And he takes as great a ransom as he can from him. Can he do this without reproach in a country in which he can wage war and one can capture another?

22. Charny asks: There are two companions who are at war, and one of them is a much closer neighbor to you than the other, but you are not involved in their war. So it happens that the one who is your closer neighbor requires you to aid him in defending his house which will be assaulted on the morrow, and you go there that evening. His enemy comes to attack the house; and you help to defend it as well as you are able without letting them down. And they fail to take the house and retreat; and attackers remain behind, dead and wounded, and all those who could go, go. And the companion who has come to defend the house of his neighbor goes to his own house. Soon after the enemy of his neighbor comes to attack him and takes prisoners and other goods and leads them away. This companion says that he has been attacked improperly and without defiance, and since he did not go out, there is no war. The other says there is. Many arguments are given on either side. How will it be judged by the law of deeds of arms?

23. Charny asks: And if by chance it was judged that the companion above was not at all nor should be at war for defending the house of his neighbor, since he was not armed except in the house. What if he went out of his fortress to attack them at a distance with his lance or on horseback and yet he did not do any damage, and he retreated back in the fortified house. Would he be able to say with reason that he was not at war?

24. Charny asks: Two lords are at war with one another and border on each other on many different frontiers. So it happens that they make general truces for their war without excepting any of the frontiers. So it happens that the truces are broken on one or two of the frontiers between these two lords, and their men-at-arms take cities and castles and do many things in the field in these marches. So should they hold to the truces, or should they be at war, although they have not yet done any damage against the others, and the truces are broken as said above?

25. Charny asks: In so far as there are two types of war, and the one kind should be fought differently than the other, as some say. One kind is *guerre guerriable,* which takes place as a dispute from one frontier to another in disdain of one lord for another, and which often is

able to move from one frontier to another in a variety of ways. The other kind of war is the desire to conquer a country, which one claims as lord but another lord holds. And this kind of war of conquest ought not to be waged. Some say war is more suitable in the manner of guerre guerriable. And so I ask how a war of conquest ought to be conducted.

26. Charny asks: A captain is besieging a city with a great number of men-at-arms; and they are well quartered just as each one should be. It happens that the captain has one of his salaried constables leave, and this constable has a good fifty men-at-arms under his banner, and they are all sent to be the garrison to defend a city of the said captain; and the constable remains there a good month or at least three weeks. And straightaway as he leaves the army another hired foreign constable joins the army and he has as many men-at-arms as the one who has left, and he lodges in the quarters of the one who has left by the orders of the marshal of the army. It happens that the captain of the army orders the constable who left to return. So he returns to the army, and comes to the army under orders to lodge in his original quarters, and the constable whom he finds lodged there refuses to leave. How will it be judged by the law of arms?

27. Charny asks: The lord of a country is at war with another lord of a country, and calls himself the lord of the country which the other one holds and says that he will conquer the country as being his by right. It happens that this lord besieges a city which belongs to the lord and to the country of which the other lord demands as his right, and maintains his siege there for a year and more. And there are spent great expenses and great costs and great efforts and great hardships, to the point that the city can no longer hold out. It happens that the lord of the country where the city is gathers together his people to rescue it if he is able; and when he is close to the city he finds that the lord who has besieged the city to be so strong in his army from ditches, walls, and palisades that in no way can he recover his city nor break the army, which is to his great disadvantage. So he requires the lord who is besieging the city to come fight him in the open field, and he will immediately put at stake possession of the city and all the goods within it. And he makes known to him that there is no better way for him to conquer the country that he claims than to fight him who holds it now. And, more, he makes known to him that he will give the place to him in common so that neither will have an advantage over the other, in regards either to the dependencies of the town or of the place itself. And he makes it known to him that when he calls himself lord of the country which is not his that he will not be able to refuse him if he wishes to conquer it. And the lord who is before the city responds that when he has taken the city, and he does not think he will fail to take it before he leaves, then he will willingly fight him, but not otherwise. So it should be decided which is more honorable: either to refuse battle against him who holds the country which he calls himself lord and conqueror and remain before the city until he has taken it, or to go from it and fight in the manner which is described above, especially when he has enough men-at-arms and foot to fight if he wishes?

28. Charny asks: There is a battle between two captains in which one party is defeated and many of the party are dead, concerning whom some say that some of those who are dead are not dead so much as defeated; and many others say of those who are dead that they are dead and defeated. How can this be?

29. Charny asks: There is a battle as above in which there are many captured, concerning whom some say that although they are captured, they do not regard them as defeated; and

there are many others who consider that those who are taken are defeated as well as captured. How can this be?

30. Charny asks: There is a battle as above in which many men-at-arms of the defeated party depart and go away. Some consider that these have gone on their honor without being defeated; and many others consider that those who have gone are defeated. How can this be?

31. Charny asks: A captain of men-at-arms rides out in the field and orders some of his scouts to see the situation of his enemies who are in the field; and these scouts are among the more capable of his people. And at the approach of their enemies one party of their enemies pursues them as fast as they can go; and the scouts retreat from their enemies and are able to retreat without loss. So there are some of the scouts who turn back and meet their enemies, and perform arms like good people should; and others retreat to their captain and make their report. Which of these are to be more valued and praised: those who went back to their lord or those who are praised?

32. Charny asks: A captain with all his army is lodged in the field or country of his enemy; and when evening comes the constables and the marshal go to set the guard for the horse and the foot; and they show them where they ought to hold themselves and remain. And since in the night their enemies attack the army of the other party where no one was on guard and they kill and take prisoner a great number of the people of the army; and the army is on the point of being defeated, but nevertheless it is not. However they lead away a great number of prisoners, horses, and goods without loss; and great damage is done to the army through death and other things, and they retreat to whence they came. The guard of this army did not ever move themselves from where they had been ordered to be, nor did they do anything. And so some say that if the guard had rescued them, their enemies would not have got away. Which should be more praised: to remain in their ordained place in the manner described above, or to have come to the rescue of the army in such need as described above? What do you think is better and more honorable?

33. Charny asks: There is a captain of war who rides out to fight his enemies; so he procures two capable men-at-arms to be under his authority and act as bodyguards. And they declare themselves willing and come to an agreement with him. It happens that in the battle one them has two of his brothers with him, and the two brothers advance in such a way that they are knocked down right next to the captain. And they are well able to be rescued by their brother who is under the authority of the lord mentioned above, and it looks indeed that he is able to rescue them if he wishes to go over there; but he doesn't know at all whether he will be able to find his lord again in good condition. Which would be the better thing to do, allow his brothers to be killed, or to rescue them and put his master in danger of not being found again? Which do you judge to be better and more honorable?

34. Charny asks: A captain of war has a castle to protect, which is right on the border with his enemies and in great danger of siege. So there are many who request the captain to be the guardian of this castle and captain, which castle ought to have at least a hundred men-at-arms and two hundred sergeants for the guard and defense of the castle. And the captain of the war answers that the one who knows best how to ask for what he will need for a year in the castle, how much he needs to live, how much artillery and other things to guard and defend the castle, as well as for the men mentioned above, to this captain he will give the guardianship of the castle and deliver all those things and pay him for a year. And if there is

anything lacking in his request, and the castle has to surrender, the castellan will pay him damages. What might he need that I don't know?

35. Charny asks: Two knights find themselves together in a secure place, and they have lords who are at war with one another. So words arise between them, for one says to the other that his lord's cause is a bad one, and the other responds to him that he lies evilly and that he will prove it with his body against his. And over these words they make an oath and swear to each other to be at a certain day, place and hour to fight to the end of the hour. And when it comes to the day, the one defending the quarrel of his master comes in the field on the named day, early in the morning, and sends an urgent request to the other that he would come forth to keep his oath to fight, just as he has promised. The other answers that he will not come; once again the first knight sends word, and the other responds as before with no other reason, so that the knight who remains in the field from morning to evening returns with the other in great default. And the next day the knight wishes for advice; can he claim the other to be defeated and as prisoner, since he did not come as he swore, and gave no legal excuse. If this comes to be judged, what will be said about his captivity or otherwise by the law of arms?

36. Charny asks: Two captains of countries are at war; one of the captains gains from the other a castle or city with great effort and expense. Which ought to have the greater desire: he who has gained it to know that it is well guarded, or he who has lost it to know it is well regained?

37. Charny asks: I have heard it said that one is able to leave and retreat from a battle from the defeated side, if he has acted in the field in seven ways without being killed or taken, without being reproached. How can this be and what are the seven ways?

38. Charny asks: A war leader rides out with a great many men-at-arms, and the leader aforesaid gives an order that all his men-at-arms under him as captain should dismount with him to fight his enemies, who are close before him ready to fight. So they get down from their horses to the ground in company with their captain, but many others are unwilling to dismount. So they fight and defeat their enemies and take possession of the field. Those who remained on their horses have had many of their horses killed in this battle. The next day these claim recompense from the captain for their horses; the captain says he is not obliged to pay it. Many good arguments are put forward on either side. How will it be judged by the law of arms?

39. Charny asks: When a man-at-arms has performed in such a way that he is considered to be good in this profession, if he finds himself armed in a place where men-at-arms are fighting and leaves, fleeing to his dishonor, what is necessary for him to repair and recover his honor? Is it necessary for him to do as much as he has done before or more, or what?

40. Charny asks: A garrison of men-at-arms is in a city under one captain. One part of the men-at-arms of the garrison leave with permission of the captain and win many prisoners and other goods and come back to their city. Those in the city who remained on guard in the city claim a share with the others. Those who were outside refuse. There are many good reasons given on either side. What will be judged by the law of arms?

41. Charny asks: Sixty or eighty men-at-arms leave by agreement and in a common undertaking from a city where they are to ride out, and say nothing else about it. So they leave before day and one of the parties of this group of men-at-arms gets lost; and one party gains a lot,

and the others gain nothing and so they find each other at the end of the day at the city. Those who have not gained anything demand a share and the others say no. And there are many good reasons offered on either side. What will be judged by the law of arms?

42. Charny asks: So a hundred or a hundred and twenty men-at-arms from the garrison of a city leave, all in one common undertaking to go attack a city of their enemies. So they ride out at night, during which one party of them loses track of the others; and the others find themselves in the morning before the city of their enemies. And their enemies see them, so they sally out and fight with those who have come before them and defeat them and take possession of the field and lead their prisoners and their people inside their city. Then those of the defeated company who were lost in the night approach the place where their companions were lost and learn about the defeat. So they undertake among themselves that they should not retreat to their city before they have done some damage to their enemies. So they remain a good three days and in these three days gain good prisoners and many other goods and return to their city with all their gains. Many of the prisoners, in other words their companions who were lost, come back, some on their faith, some on a bond, and demand a share of the gains which their companions have made; and their companions say no. Many good arguments are given either side. How will it be judged by the law of arms?

43. Charny asks: Men-at-arms from a city garrison leave to ride against their enemies without the permission of their captain and lose many of their horses. And they come back into their city and demand compensation for their horses which they have lost, and the captain says no. How will it etc.?

44. Charny asks: And if the men-at-arms mentioned above gain much and lose nothing, those of the city who remained to guard and defend it demand a share, and those who rode out say no. Many good arguments are made on either side. How will it be judged by the law of arms?

Answer: Those who remained in the city will have nothing if there was not a previous agreement that everything was in shares, and this is right and reasonable.

45. Charny asks: So men-at-arms ride out against their enemies and all promise to take booty together in the field. So it happens that they fight and are on the point of being defeated and killed; and many of them are taken and some of them leave. But chance brings about in the end that those who were losing at first defeat the others and kill and capture and gain much, and take possession of the field. When they are all at the hotel they bring their booty and come to share it out, some of those who left come to the booty to have a share; and the others say no. How should it be according to the law of arms?

46. Charny asks: Men-at-arms leave a place to ride against their enemies and when they are in the field they promise each other to collect booty in common and share it out. So they ride out and fight and defeat their enemies and gain horses, harness, and money and plenty of other goods, and a large number of good prisoners. And when it comes to share booty, each brings his gains except for the prisoners. So many demand that the prisoners should go into the common booty; and others say no. How should it be judged by the law of arms?

47. Charny asks: Part of a garrison of a city, a hundred or a hundred and twenty men-at-arms, depart on an enterprise by agreement, including booty in common. So they ride out of the city to attack their enemies' country; and in riding at night one of the

companions, with ten men of arms from among the companions, by chance loses the rest. And when he sees that he has lost track of the others, he returns to the city which he left and disarms himself and feeds his horses and then mounts his horse. After he has eaten in the said city he rides out alone with his companions and gains prisoners, horses, spoils and many other goods, and takes all his gains to safety in the city from which he came. And he finds the others in whose company he first set out from the city, who have gained in the same manner a great deal from their enemies. So the companion with the ten men-at-arms demands his share of booty from the companions in whose company he had set out with in the morning and whom he had lost track of. In annoyance the other companions say no. Many good arguments are made on either side. What will be said about it by men-at-arms?

48. Charny asks: If it was said by the men-at-arms that these companions had common booty with those with whom they had left in the morning, the others would also want to demand for the common booty that which the companions gained after they left the city, after the repast that they had in the city. And the companions say no for all the good reasons that are able to be used by one party or the other. What will be decided about it by men-at-arms?

49. Charny asks: A captain of men-at-arms in a castle sends a man-at-arms from his hired soldiers from the said castle out of the castle for the common needs of the castle and of the companions of the captain of the country to have the pillage of the said garrison. And the garrison remains and the said man-at-arms remain in the city where the captain of the country is, to await the pillage. And as it happens that the captain of the country rides out and the said man-at-arms with him so that they encounter their enemies in the field, and as it is they come to close combat with their enemies. Part of the garrison of the castle from which the man-at-arms has left knows about this expedition, so they move up to the place of battle without the knowledge of the captain of the country. And their enemies are defeated, and the men-at-arms who have overcome them gain prisoners and plenty of goods and take possession of the field. The captain of the country goes back to the city from which he left and the same evening also the man-at-arms mentioned above who was with him for the business of the pillage aforesaid. And the men of the garrison of the castle mentioned above return to the said castle with all their gains. The said man-at-arms returns to the same castle the next day from the business and claims a share of the booty with the other companions of the castle who have been in the affair, since an ordinance had been made in the castle that none should have a share of booty except those who rode out. And those in the garrison say no. Many good reasons are given on either side. How will it be judged by the law of arms?

50. Charny asks: Since on the day of the battle the captain of the country has said and ordained that all who ride in his company on that day take common shares in all the booty, and the men-at-arms of the garrison of the castle who have ridden out in the company of the captain of the country demand part of the said booty, notwithstanding the share which he claims with his companions of the garrison of the said castle. Will he take a share of the said booty?

51. Charny asks: If it is said that the man-at-arms takes a share in the booty with his companions of the garrison of the said castle, and also that he takes a share of the booty of the captain of the country, the companions of the garrison of the castle who have ridden

out demand shares in the share which the said man-at-arms has taken in the booty of the captain of the country. The man-at-arms says no. Many good arguments are given on either side. How will it be judged by the law of arms?

52. Charny asks: Two captains fight each other in the field with a great number of men-at-arms on either side. So one of the captains orders that all the gains which one part or the other has on the day should be common booty. So they ride out to fight, and when they come to the battle many of the men of the captain who has made this order leave the field and flee. And indeed though they did not remain, the said captain defeats his enemies and gains prisoners and plenty of other goods and takes possession of the field. And when they have returned to their position, those who fled have returned, too, and demand a share of the booty with the others. The others say no. Many good arguments are given on either side. How will it be judged by the law of arms?

53. Charny asks: Some men of a castle garrison ride out and encounter their enemies; and they fight and the enemies are defeated. The men of the said garrison gain prisoners, horses, and plenty of other goods, and take possession of the field. So they return to their castle, and all their gains of whatever sort are part of the common booty by the ordinance made and enforced in their castle. So it happens that before the gains have been shared out their enemies ride out, and the men know of it and ride out and encounter them. One of the men-at-arms of the garrison has gone out, mounted on a horse which he has gained on the day before with his companions and is part of the booty, and in that expedition he loses that horse. When they have returned to their castle and want to divide up their gains, the companions demand their share of the horse which was lost. The man-at-arms who lost it says no. How will it be judged?

54. Charny asks: A captain of a city has retained a gentleman at the wages of a foot sergeant. So the captain and the people under him agree that all who take profit from their enemies will put into the common booty for the men-at-arms to share, and that and the footmen will have a share of it, but less than the men-at-arms. So it happens that the men-at-arms and the footmen of this garrison sally out against their enemies and kill and take and gain a great deal. The gentleman who is at the wages of a footman has found a horse and is mounted on that day with the others who are well armed. When they have returned they share the booty; and this gentleman demands the share of a man-at-arms, and the men-at-arms say no. Many good arguments are given on either side. How will it be judged by the law of arms?

55. Charny asks: The captain of a place leaves it and rides out against his enemies, and he has made an ordinance that all should share in the booty in common whatever they gain. And they ride until they see their enemies. So the captain orders that all should dismount to fight on foot against their enemies; many dismount and many remain on horseback. Those who are on foot with their captain attack their enemies and defeat them. When it comes to the defeat, those on horse join those on foot who have already defeated the enemy. When evening comes, those on horse demand a share of the common booty, and those who have dismounted say no. How will it be judged by the men-at-arms?

56. Charny asks: Men-at-arms ride out and encounter each other and fight. One of the men-at-arms in one party strikes his spurs to save himself, and three of the other side pursue him. The first stops him with the bridle, and he does not want to surrender to him. The second takes him by the head and holds a knife at his throat, and again he does not wish to

surrender to him. The third comes after and tells him to surrender to him, and that man-at-arms surrenders himself to the third. When in the evening each of the three uses all the good arguments he knows, and there are plenty, that this prisoner ought to belong to him. Who will have him, and how will it be judged by the law of arms?

57. Charny asks: Men-at-arms encounter each other and fight. One of the men-at-arms in one party takes one from the other side, and that one surrenders himself as prisoner by his good faith, if the other protects him from death; and the one who takes him promises him and then leaves him unguarded. So it happens that some of the men-at-arms of the same party as he who took the prisoner find this prisoner and tell him that if he does not surrender he will die, and he answers that he has surrendered to one of their party and gives his name. They don't believe him and strike him and wound him in many places and want to kill him if he does not surrender, and during this conflict the prisoner is rescued by his party and is led off to safety. The one who first captured him requires him to come to him as a captive according to the faith which he gave; and the other says that he is not required to do so. Many good arguments are given on either side. How should the men-at-arms judge the case?

58. Charny asks: Two captains of war are in the field against each other and fight. One of the parties has the better of it at the beginning, so that those in this party take ten or twelve prisoners. In the end it happens that the party of the prisoners rally and attack the others and defeat them entirely and take possession of the field and recover all the other prisoners taken at the beginning. And so those who took the first prisoners that they should come and be their prisoners; some of those who took the first prisoners are taken themselves and some have gone. It was said to the first prisoners: "Swear to be my prisoner," and so they did it and should not be contesting this captivity. The first say that they are not required to go, and the others say that they are. There are many good arguments. How should it be judged by the law of arms?

59. Charny asks: A prisoner is taken in the field and he is a man-at-arms and it is required that he swear to be a prisoner and he does it. And he leads him into the city and puts him under guard without asking any other faith. And he escapes the next day and gets himself to safety. Can he do this without reproach?

60. Charny asks: One man-at-arms has another as his prisoner and makes him swear that he will hold himself in captivity within the gates of the city and allows his prisoner to go through the city; and the prisoner swears this and loyally keeps his word. Afterwards it happens that the master of this prisoner puts him in a house in the city and forbids and commands him not to leave it without permission and without renewing his oath. And two or three days after the prohibition the prisoner escapes and gets himself to safety. His master requires him to return; the prisoner refuses. Many good arguments are given on either side. How will it be judged by the law of arms?

61. Charny asks: A man-at-arms holds another as prisoner and it is agreed that the ransom will be put in the hand of the master without any further word being said at a certain place and day. The prisoner comes to his place and time provided with his ransom, but he finds that his master has been dead for some time. So he remains there the whole day; and they take him before the heir of his master and demand the money from the prisoner. The prisoner says that he is not required to give it. Many good arguments are given on either side. How will it be judged by the law of arms?

62. Charny asks: So it happens that a man-at-arms has taken another and he holds the other as a prisoner and makes the prisoner swear that he will return within a certain period to a castle which he names; and he swears to do this. The prisoner comes to the castle and finds that the people of his party have recently taken the castle. The prisoner enters and says that he has come to keep his faith. Those inside do not want to take him prisoner. Nevertheless he remains in the castle eight days or more and no one claims anything from him; so he goes back to his house. Then the master comes and claims him as his prisoner, and the prisoner says no. Many good arguments are given on either side. How will it be judged by the law of arms?

63. Charny asks: A man-at-arms puts another to ransom to be paid over three or four installments; and the prisoner promises to do all in his power fulfill it, or to return. The prisoner comes at the first term and pays up; at the second term he returns to prison because he can't pay. The master imposes a very big ransom which he did not impose before because the prisoner wasn't able to pay the second installment. The prisoner says that his ransom ought not to increase. Many good arguments are given on either side. How will it be judged by the law of arms?

64. Charny asks: A man-at-arms holds another as his prisoner and makes him give his faith that he will not leave a house where he will put him without permission. And then it happens that the master becomes angry with his prisoner and strikes and beats him. After this the prisoner escapes and goes his way. His master claims him; the prisoner says no. Many good arguments are given on either side. How will it be judged by the law of arms?

65. Charny asks: A knight or a squire is angry with another so that the one speaks words of defiance to the other, and the one who has been defied finds himself at that moment the stronger. So he takes him immediately to his place without more delay and leads him away and ransoms him. Is he able to do this, at least in a country where one is allowed to take others as prisoners, for the one who made the defiance was not permitted to attack the other on the day of the defiance but not until the next day.

66. Charny asks: A man-at-arms holds another as prisoner; the one who is taken has permission from his master to send out for robes and other things which he wants for his comfort, like dishes and goblets of silver, and some precious things. The prisoner's master takes these things into his possession and says that they will be his; the prisoner says no, it is not fitting. Many good arguments are given on either side. How will it be judged by the law of arms?

67. Charny asks: Two captains fight each other and one knight or squire takes another, and this one surrenders himself as a prisoner and surrenders his sword to him. No one asks for him to give his faith and he does not give it. And the one who is taken looks over the field, sees his advantage, and strikes his spurs and thus goes his way. Tell me if he is able to do this without reproach, for the way in which he had been defeated?

68. Charny asks: A man-at-arms takes another man-at-arms by some warlike deed and leads him off to a city where he remains in garrison. So the master makes the prisoner swear that he will be a loyal prisoner in this city, within the gates, and he gives his faith in this manner. The master goes outside the city, and before he is able to return the city is taken by some enemies, the friends of the prisoner. The prisoner goes home. The one who took him requires him to come to him on his faith as his prisoner. The other

refuses. Many good arguments are given on either side. How will it be judged by the law of arms?

69. Charny asks: Men-at-arms encounter each other in the field and fight; and one of the parties is defeated. It happens that one of the knights or squires of the defeated party is strongly attacked by many others. And of those who attack him there is one who says to him, "Surrender yourself," and the knight asks him if he is a gentleman, and the other tells him "yes." And the knight says "I surrender to you if you are a gentleman." And the other responds, "I take you as a gentleman," and thus takes him away to the city. And when the knight is in the city, he asks and learns that the one who captured him is nothing but a sergeant and no gentleman. Now the knight comes to the captain and to the people who are in the city and says that he is not the prisoner of the sergeant. How will it be judged by the law of arms?

70. Charny asks: If it was said that the knight or squire should not remain prisoner of the sergeant, will he go free or will he remain prisoner, and whose? How will it be judged by the law of arms?

71. Charny asks: A man-at-arms has made another his prisoner in proper warfare. So they agree that the prisoner's ransom is to be paid at a certain time if the prisoner is able, and the prisoner remains near his master under by his faith without any other captivity. So one day the master comes to the prisoner and swears on the holy gospels and similar things that if he does not pay his ransom at the term, when the term is past the master will cut off his head. And about this time news comes to the prisoner that he will not be able to pay his ransom. So he begs his master to lengthen the term and the master is not willing and swears as before. What ought the prisoner do? Is he able to go without evil reproach?

72. Charny asks: A man-at-arms has taken another prisoner in a deed of war. It happens that the prisoner puts himself to ransom with the agreement of his master for a certain sum to be paid on a set day, and if he does not pay he will return to captivity as if he had never set a ransom. And after this agreement is made, and when the day comes the prisoner comes to his master and gives him money for his ransom, but he is not able to find any more. And the master takes this money and gives his prisoner permission and a new day to pay the remainder. The prisoner leaves and comes back and brings nothing with him, for he is not able to do so, and his master says that he will set him a very great ransom, which he had not done before. The prisoner says he is not able to do this nor ought he. The master says that he can. They submit the dispute to the law of arms. How will it be judged?

73. Charny asks: Because there are many who are involved in two equal wars, I ask that if this one is taken by his enemies in one of the wars and put to ransom and one gives him permission on his faith to come back personally carrying his ransom on the day that the one has given him and so he is not able to until after this day. And in the meantime the enemy from the other war encounters him and takes him and wants to put him to ransom, and he wants to be paid before the other. And the other who had first captured him says that he should not do it. Many good reasons are given on either side. How will it be judged by the law of arms?

74. Charny asks: A man-at-arms has taken another in war; it happens that the master has set a certain ransom with the agreement of the prisoner, either to pay on a set day or to return to

his captivity on that day. And one of the party of the prisoner's master takes himself to the master as pledge to pay for the prisoner or instead of him surrender himself on the set day. And in the meantime it is made known by the counsel of the pledges that the prisoner is divested himself of all his heritage, all that he had, into the hands of his heirs. And then the pledge leads back the prisoner on the agreed day and asks the prisoner's master that he be released from his status as pledge. The master says no, for he has not fulfilled his captivity as he agreed to do. Many good reasons are given on either side. How will it be judged by the law of arms?

75. Charny asks: Men-at-arms encounter each other and fight until one of the parties is defeated. It happens that one man-at-arms of the party with the upper hand takes a man-at-arms of the defeated party and says to him, "Surrender to me!" And the man-at-arms says "I surrender to you," and gives him his sword; and the one who has captured him gives him to one of his valets to guard and this companion goes to fight with the others. Then another of those who have the upper hand comes and finds the prisoner which the valet of the other companion is guarding and demands from him whose prisoner he is, and the prisoner responds, "So and so of your party." The man-at-arms asks if he has given his faith, and the prisoner replies that he has not given any faith, at which the companion says that he will kill him if he does not swear to be his prisoner. And this one takes his oath as a prisoner and takes him away despite the valet. And when evening comes the companion who first took him without faith being pledged demands his prisoner; the other who has his faith says no. Many good arguments are given on either side. How will it be judged by judgment of arms?

76. Charny asks: A man-at-arms takes another in a deed of war and the master says to his prisoner that he will set a ransom, and the prisoner offers a thousand écus and his master agrees. And when the prisoner is put to ransom and agreed with his master, another friend of the prisoner's master comes and begs that he will give him possession of the prisoner to deal with at his pleasure, and the master grants his request and releases the prisoner from his oath and makes him give his oath to him to whom he has granted him. And the one to whom he has given the prisoner imposes on him a ransom of 4000 écus, and the prisoner who has no choice agrees and pays them so that he has acquitted himself of the 4000 écus and his faith. So the prisoner comes and pursues his first master to give him the surplus over the 1000 écus that he had given as a ransom, which surplus amounted to 3000 écus. And the first master responds that these agreements were never written down or sworn, and the prisoner says that [the other agreement] had no force, for it was between him and the other. Many good arguments are made on one side or the other. How will it be judged by the law of arms?

77. Charny asks: A man-at-arms is taken by his enemies in a set battle, and he who has taken him and to whom he has surrendered himself leads him to his lodgings, then puts a ransom on him and sets a term to pay his ransom, and makes him swear that he will not arm himself nor carry arms before he has completed his ransom. And the prisoner departs according to his agreement to raise the ransom and during the term and settlement he arms himself with his people and it happens that he fights against those whose prisoner he was before. And again they are defeated and it happens that the aforesaid prisoner is taken by another of the party of his master to whom he was prisoner before and leads him off to safety. And when evening comes the first master of the said prisoner demands the prisoner

for himself and says that he ought not to be the prisoner of the other before he is quits with him. And the other says that he has taken the prisoner as a man-at-arms and by force of arms and that he ought to remain his prisoner, with other good arguments on one side and the other. How will it be judged by the law of arms?

78. Charny asks: Since some contend that when a man-at-arms who is captured in the field, armed in a *besoigne* and the man-at-arms says "I surrender" or gives his faith, that this ought to be a reproach of cowardice to him, how can he be captured and keep his honor and without reproach?

79. Charny asks: Since I do not understand when a man-at-arms surrenders himself into the hands of his enemies in a set-piece affair (*besoigne arrestee*) in what way he can say the words, "I surrender," which will not be considered cowardice, I ask to be enlightened, for I don't understand it.

80. Charny asks: Men-at-arms have fought against each other until one of the parties is defeated. It happens that one man-at-arms takes as prisoner a man-at-arms of the defeated party, and the prisoner surrenders to the man-at-arms who guards him as he can to save him. And then comes a man-at-arms of the same party and affinity of the one who has taken the prisoner and says he will kill the prisoner. The one who has taken him tells him that the prisoner has surrendered to him and tells and entreats him not to kill him. The other does not believe him, and kills him. The next day the one who has captured the prisoner takes the one who killed him as his prisoner and takes him without any further defiance and puts him to ransom for as much as he can. And the other says as an excuse that the first cannot take him or ransom him in this manner, while the one who has taken him says he will do it. How will it be judged by the law of arms?

80A. Charny asks: Men-at-arms fight in the field against their enemies and it happens that one of the men-at-arms who has the upper hand takes another man-at-arms and he who is taken surrenders to the one who has taken him and gives his faith as his prisoner. But very soon the party of the prisoner has the better of it and defeats the others and takes the field, and the prisoner who sees his party get the upper hand attacks his enemies and takes two or three of them and makes them swear to be prisoners and gives them a day to return. Those come on their day and demand of the captain of the one to whom they have sworn by the law of arms, saying that they should not be held to be prisoners to him who on that day was a prisoner, notwithstanding that he is able to argue that because of the rescue he ought to be free; and the first one taken says that they are his prisoners, for he was rescued. And many good arguments are given on one side or the other. How will it be judged by the law of arms?

81. Charny asks: A man-at-arms takes another in a set battle and tells him, "Surrender," and the other answers, "I won't because I am the prisoner of such and such," and gives a name. And the one who seized him says, "Give me your faith that you are the prisoner of the one you name," and he gives his faith that such is the case, and the other frees him. When evening comes that one [i.e. the captor] who knows that he was the prisoner of the other speaks to him [i.e. the first supposed captor] and this one, who knows nothing of it, nor has taken the prisoner, nor even seen him during the whole day, says he would like to claim him as his prisoner, and so he does it. And the prisoner says no and that he only did it to save himself. Many good arguments are given on one side or another. How will it be judged by the law of arms?

82. Charny asks: A man-at-arms takes another in a besoigne arrestee in the field and says to him, "Surrender." "Willingly," the other says, "but you must promise to protect me." And the captor responds, "Swear to be my prisoner and I promise to save you," and the other gives his faith on that condition. So it happens that another man-at-arms from the party of the one who has taken the prisoner finds that prisoner without an escort, so he attacks him and says to him, "Surrender." The prisoner responds "I won't, because I have given my faith to such and such of your party and I will swear to that if you wish." "No," says the other, "surrender yourself to me or you are dead," and attacks him; and the prisoner says, "I surrender," and gives his faith and this one leads him to the lodgings. When evening comes the one who first took the prisoner comes to the other who later retook this prisoner and demands the prisoner as his own, and the second who took him says no, the prisoner ought to be his. There are many things said on one side and the other. How will it be judged by the law of arms?

83. Charny asks: Men-at-arms ride out to fight each other. Which is better if they are to profit from the day's fighting: to put everything as booty in common, or to have each one keep the prisoners and other things he happens to get?

84. Charny asks: Two men-at-arms find themselves afoot in the field, and they are enemies. The one is armed entirely as appertains to a man-at-arms and has his sword and knife. The other is unarmed in his tunic but he has, clearly to be seen on his hood, some precious stones that he was willing to put there, but no weapon nor any other armor. And there they are going to fight to the death. Which of these two would you rather be?

85. Charny asks: A hundred men-at-arms are in the field all prepared to fight against a hundred others, all of them as good and as well mounted as they are, and the horses on either side are completely armed, and well covered, because they have promised to fight on their horses as long as their horses can last, if they are not killed at the hands of their enemies, and without any advantage from deceit. One of the parties does not have any weapons except for their hands, but they have good spurs on their feet; those in the other party each have a good sword in their hands but no other weapons, but they have no spurs and can't get any. Which of these would you rather be?

86. Charny asks: There are two cities which are at war with each other and in each there is a garrison of a hundred men-at-arms, all good companions and skilled men. And near these two cities is a good city that is not at war, but which has in it as many handsome and lively damsels as in any city one knows. So it happens that each of the men-at-arms in the two cities for their virtues has a ladylove who pleases him in this good city and it seems to each of them that his ladylove is the best and most beautiful of them all. So it happens that the ladyloves of the companions in one of the two cities send letters to them and make it known that they should come the next day to them to amuse them and dance and lead a good life. And the companions get up early in the morning and wish to take part in the great joy, celebration, and welcome which is made for them. It is hardly necessary to speak of how each one in her own right jokes, talks, sings, and dances all day and all night so very honorably as ladies ought to know how to for those who are their friends. And when the morning comes the companions wish to arm for their departure, but the ladies do not permit any to give them a hand in arming except themselves, and each of them helps the one she loves best. And at their departure each lady has kissed her own friend and given him a ring or other jewel and they beg them to fight well for the love of them. And the men give

their faith by St. John and then go. So it happens that the ladies and ladyloves of the other companions know of the good time which the others have had; so they each have written in their own hand a letter to their friends telling them that they should come to them immediately and they will enjoy such a good time that they will leave them well content and that the ladies are well prepared to put on such a good time as was ever done. The companions of the other city mount up, completely armed, happy and in great joy to go to their ladies, because of the good news they have just received. So they go into the field and when they come to the city they see the companions who are coming from their ladies. So they ride against each other to fight. Of which party would you prefer to be, as having a better will to fight well?

87. Charny asks: Fifty knights have taken it upon themselves to fight against a hundred on a certain named day; and the day of the battle comes. The fifty defeat the hundred and many deeds of arms are done by either party. Which would you prefer: to be considered the best knight of the hundred or the worst of the fifty in respect of this day?

88. Charny asks: Which ought to have the more doubt and fear? The one who is considered to be moderately brave, or the one who is considered an inordinate coward?

89. Charny asks: Which would you prefer: that of all the days of arms which you have had or think to have, that in half of the days you should have the prize in the fighting over the others and you are taken to be of no account in the other half; or that in all of the days which you have had and think to have you will gain great renown, but you will get no prize from your good deeds.

90. Charny asks: Which would you prefer: intelligence or prowess?

91. Charny asks: Which would you prefer: That you were considered of no account in regard to arms in war, and in all the deeds of arms of peace where you have been or you will ever be, you have the day and you have the prize; or that in all the deeds of arms of war where you have been present and you will be in the future, you have been and will be on all those days considered to be one of those who did well with no other prize, and in deeds of arms of peace you are considered of no account.

92. Charny asks: Which makes more sense in making war: to know well how to flee or to know well how to pursue?

93. Charny asks: Two captains fight in the field together with all their people. So it happens that one of the parties has many who leave without striking a blow and many others who in the clash surrender without striking a blow. Which give greater heart to their enemies and greater discomfiture to their friends: those who surrender without striking a blow or those who leave without striking a blow?

ORDINANCES OF RICHARD II[1]

These are the Statutes, Ordonnances, and Customs, to be observed in the Army, ordained and made by good consultation and deliberation of our most Excellent Lord the King Richard, John Duke of Lancaster, Seneschal of England, Thomas Earl of Essex, and Buckingham, Constable of England, and Thomas de Mowbray Earl of Nottingham, Marshal of England, and other Lords, Earls, Barons, Bannereтts, and experienced Knights, whom they have thought proper to call unto them; then being at Durham the 17th Day of the Month of July, in the ninth Year of the Reign of our Lord the King Richard II.

I. FIRSTLY. That all manner of, of what nation, state, or condition they may be, shall be obedient to our lord the king, to his constable and marshal, under penalty of every thing they can forfeit in body and goods.

II. ITEM, that none be so hardy as to touch the body of our lord, nor the vessel in which it is contained, under pain of being drawn, hanged, and beheaded.

III. ITEM, that none be so hardy as to rob and pillage the church, nor to destroy any man belonging to holy church, religious or otherwise, nor any woman, nor to take them prisoners, if not bearing arms; nor to force any woman, upon pain of being hanged.

IV. ITEM, that no one be so hardy to go before, or otherwise than in the battle to which he belongs, under the banner or pennon of his lord or master, except the herbergers, whose names shall be given in by their lords or masters to our constable and marshal, upon pain of losing their horses.

V. ITEM, that no one take quarters, otherwise than by the assignment of the constable and marshal and the herbergers; and that, after the quarters are assigned and delivered, let no one be so hardy as to remove himself, or quit his quarters, on any account whatsoever, under pain of forfeiture of horse and armor, and his body to be in arrest, and at the king's will.

VI. ITEM, that every one be obedient to his captain, and perform watch and ward, forage, and all other things belonging to his duty, under penalty of losing his horse and armor, and his body being in arrest to the marshal, till he shall have made his peace with his lord or master, according to the award of the court.

VII. ITEM, that no one be so hardy as to rob or pillage another of money, victuals, provisions, forage, or any other thing, on pain of losing his head; nor shall any one take any victuals, merchandise, or any other thing whatsoever, brought for the refreshment of the army, under the same penalty; and any one who shall give the names of such robbers and pillagers to the constable and marshal, shall have twenty nobles for his labor.

VIII. ITEM, no one shall make a riot or contention in the army for debate of arms, prisoners, lodgings, or any other thing whatsoever, nor cause any party or assembly of persons, under pain (the principals as well as the parties) of losing their horses and armor, and having their bodies in arrest at the king's will, and if it be a boy or page he shall lose his left ear. Any person conceiving himself aggrieved shall make known his grievance to the constable and marshal, and right shall be done him.

IX. ITEM, that no one be so hardy as to make a contention or debate in the army on account of any grudge respecting time past, or for any thing to come; if in such contest or debate any one shall be slain, those who were the occasion shall be hanged; and if any one shall proclaim his own name, or that of his lord or master, so as to cause a rising of the people, whereby an affray might happen in the army, he who made the proclamation shall be drawn and hanged.

X. ITEM, that no one be so hardy as to cry "havoc," under pain of losing his head, and that he or they that shall be the beginners of the said cry shall likewise be beheaded, and their bodies afterwards be hanged up by the arms.

XI. ITEM, that no one make the cry called mount or any other whatsoever in the army, on account of the great danger that may thereby happen to the whole army; which God forbid! and that on pain, if he be a man-at-arms, or archer on horseback, of losing his best horse; and if he be an archer on foot or boy, he shall have his left ear cut off.

XII. ITEM, if in any engagement whatsoever an enemy shall be beat down to the earth, and he who shall have thus thrown him down shall go forwards in the pursuit, and any other shall come afterwards, and shall take the faith or parole of the said enemy, he shall have half of the said prisoner, and he who overthrew him the other half; but he who received his parole shall have the keeping of him, giving security to his partner.

XIII. ITEM, if any one takes a prisoner, and another shall join him, demanding a part, threatening that otherwise he will kill him (the prisoner), he shall have no part, although the share be granted to him; and if he kills the said prisoner, he shall be in arrest to the marshal, without being delivered till he has satisfied the party, and his horses and armour shall be forfeited to the constable.

XIV. ITEM, that no man go out on an expedition by night or by day, unless with the knowledge and by the permission of the chieftain of the battle in which he is, so that they may be able to succor him should occasion require it, on pain of losing horse and armor.

XV. ITEM, that for no news or affray whatsoever that may happen in the army, any one shall put himself in disarray in his battle, whether on an excursion or in quarters, unless by assignment of his chieftain, under pain of losing horse and armor.

XVI. ITEM, that every one pay to his lord or master the third of all manner of gains of arms; herein are included those who do not receive pay, but only have the benefit of quarters, under the banner or pennon of arms of a captain.

XVII. ITEM, that no one be so hardy as to raise a banner or pennon of St. George, or any other, to draw together the people out of the army, to go to any place whatsoever, under pain, that those who thus make themselves captains shall be drawn and hanged, and those who follow them be beheaded, and all their goods and heritages forfeited to the king.

XVIII. ITEM, that every man, of what estate, condition, or nation he may be, so that he be of our party, shall bear a large sign of the arms of St. George before, and another behind, upon peril that if he be hurt or slain in default thereof, he who shall hurt or slay him shall suffer no penalty for it: and that no enemy shall bear the said sign of St. George, unless he be a prisoner, upon pain of death.

XIX. ITEM, if any one shall take a prisoner, as soon as he comes to the army, he shall bring him to his captain or master on pain of losing his part to his said captain or master; and that his said captain or master shall bring him to our lord the king, constable, or marshal, as soon as he well can, without taking him elsewhere, in order that they may examine him concerning news and intelligence of the enemy, under pain of losing his third to him who may first make it known to the constable or marshal; and that every one shall guard, or cause to be guarded by his soldiers, his said prisoner, that he may not ride about at large in the army, nor shall suffer him to be at large in his quarters, without having a guard over him, left he espy the secrets of the army, under pain of losing his said prisoner; reserving to his said lord the third of the whole, if there is not a partner in the offence; and the second part to him that shall first take him; and the third part to the constable. On the like pain, and also of his body being in arrest, and at the king's will, he shall not suffer his said prisoner to go out of the army for his ransom, nor for any other cause, without leave of the king, constable, and marshal, or the commander of the battalion in which he is.

XX. ITEM, that every one shall well and duly perform his watch in the army, and with the number of men-at-arms and archers as is assigned him, and that he shall remain the full limited term, unless by the order or permission of him before whom the watch is made, on pain of having his head cut off.

XXI. ITEM, that no one shall give passports or safe conduct to a prisoner nor any other, nor leave to any enemy to come into the army, on pain of forfeiture of all his goods to the king, and his body in arrest and at his will; except our lord the King, Monsieur de Lancaster, seneschal, the constable, and marshal: and that none be so hardy as to violate the safe conduit of our lord the king, upon pain of being drawn and hanged, and his goods and heritage forfeited to the king; nor to infringe the safe-conducts of our said lord of Lancaster, seneschal, constable, and marshal, upon pain of being beheaded.

XXII. ITEM, if any one take a prisoner, he shall take his faith, and also his bascinet, or gauntlet, to be a pledge and in sign that he is so taken, or he shall leave him under the guard of some of his soldiers, under pain, that if he takes him, and does not do as is here directed, and another comes afterwards, and takes him from him (if not under a guard) as is said, his bascinet or right gauntlet in pledge, he shall have the prisoner, though the first had taken his faith.

XXIII. ITEM, that no one be so hardy to retain the servant of another, who has covenanted for the expedition, whether soldier, man-at-arms, archer, page or boy, after he shall have been challenged by his master, under pain that his body shall be in arrest till he shall have made satisfaction to the party complaining, by award of the court, and his horses and armor forfeited to the constable.

XXIV. ITEM, that no one be so hardy to go for forage before the lords or others, whosoever they may be, who mark out or assign the places for the foragers, if it is a man-at-arms, he shall lose his horses and harness to the constable, and his body shall be arrested by the marshal, and if it is a valet or boy, he shall have his left ear cut off.

XXV. THAT none be so hardy as to quarter himself otherwise than by the assignment of the herbergers, who are authorized to distribute quarters, under like penalty.

XXVI. ITEM, that every lord whatsoever cause to be delivered to the constable and marshal the names of their herbergers, under penalty, that if any one goes forward and takes quarters, and his name is not delivered in to the constable and marshal, he shall lose his horses and armor.

Endnotes

1. From Francis Grose, *Military Antiquities: Respecting a History of the English Army from the Conquest to the Present Time* (London: S. Hooper, 1801), Vol. 2, 64–69. This text follows a transcription of Will McLean's in modernizing some of Grose's spelling, and translating "mount" from the original French, which Grose retained in Article XI.

BIBLIOGRAPHY

Primary Sources

Adam Murimuth, *Continuatio Chronicarum*, in *Rerum Britannicarum Medii Aevi Scriptores* (Rolls Series), 93:123–4.

Allen, S.J. and Emilie Amt (eds.), *The Crusades: A Reader.* Peterborough, Ont.: Broadview Press, 2003.

Allmand C.T., ed. *Society at War: The Experience of England and France during the Hundred Years War.* New York: Barnes & Noble, 1973.

Bonet, Honoré. *L'Arbre des Batailles d'Honoré Bonet* [sic], ed. Ernest Nys. Brussels: N.P., 1883.

Philippe de Remi, Beaumanoir, and Amédée Salmon, *Coutumes de Beauvaisis; texte critique pub. avec une introduction, un glossaire et une table analytique.* 3 vols. Paris: A. Picard et fils, 1899.

Black Book of the Admiralty, ed. Sir Travers Twiss, 4 vols. London: Longman & Co., 1871.

Brault, Gerard J., ed. *The Song of Roland: An Analytical Edition.* 2 vols. University Park, PA: Pennsylvania State University Press, 1978.

Brush, H.R., ed. "La Bataille de trente Anglois et de trente Bretons." *Modern Philology* 9 (1911–2): 511-44; 10 (1912–3): 82–136.

Chronique de Jean le Bel, ed. Jules Viard and Eugène Déprez. 2 vols. Paris: Renouard, 1906.

Chronique du Religieux de Saint-Denys, ed. M. Bellaguet. 6 vols. Paris, 1832–52.

De controversia in curia militari inter Ricardum Le Scrope et Robertum Grosvenor milites rege Ricardo Secundo, MCCCLXXXV–MCCCXC e recordis in turre Londinensi asservatis. London: Printed by Samuel Bentley, 1832.

Geoffrey le Baker, *Chronicon Galfridi le Baker de Swynebroke*, ed. Edward Maunde Thompson. Oxford: Clarendon Press, 1889.

Giovanni da Legnano. *Tractatus de bello, de represalis, et de duello*, ed. Thomas Erskine Holland. Oxford: Oxford University Press, 1917.

History of William Marshal, ed. A. J. Holden, S. Gregory, and D. Crouch. 3 vols. ANTS Occasional Publications 4–6. London: Anglo-Norman Text Society, 2002–6.

Joustes de Saint-Inglebert, 1389–90. Poème contemporaine, ed. J. Pichon *in Partie inedite des Chronique de Saint-Denis.* Paris, N.P.: 1864.

Kaeuper, Richard W. and Elspeth Kennedy. *The Book of Chivalry of Geoffroi de Charny: Text, Context, and Translation.* Philadelphia: University of Pennsylvania Press, 1996.

King René's Tournament Book: René d'Anjou, Traictié de la forme et devis d'ung tournoy, tr. Elizabeth Bennett. N.P.: 1992. Online: http://www.princeton.edu/~ezb/rene/renehome.html, accessed January 26, 2014.

Martorell, Joanot and Martí Joan de Galba, *Tirant lo Blanc,* tr. David H. Rosenthal New York: Schocken Books, 1984.

Matthew Paris's English History, tr. J. A. Giles. 2 vols. London: Bohn, 1854.

Ordonnances des Roys de France de la troisième race vol. 4, ed. D.F. Secousse. Paris, 1734.

Roland, Ferdinand ed., *Parties inédites de l'œuvre de Sicilie, heraut d'Alphonse V roi d'Aragon, maréschal d'armes du pays de Hainaut, auteur du Blason des couleurs. Publications de la Société des Bibliophiles des Belges séant à Mons,* vol. 22. Mons, N.P.: 1867.

Rymer, T. *Foedera, Conventiones, Litterae, etc.* ed. G. Holmes, 20 vols. London, N.P.: 1704–35.

Secondary Sources

Ayton, Andrew. *Knights and Warhorses: Military Service and the English Aristocracy under Edward III.* Woodbridge: Boydell Press, 1994.

Ayton, Andrew and J. L. Price, eds. *The Medieval Military Revolution: State, Society and Military Change in Medieval and Early Modern Europe.* London and New York: I. B. Tauris, 1995.

Barber, Richard and Juliet R. V. Barker. *Tournaments: Jousts, Chivalry and Pageants in the Middle Ages.* Woodbridge: Boydell Press, 1989.

Barker, Juliet R.V. *The Tournament in England 1100–1400.* Woodbridge: Boydell Press, 1986.

Bonet, Honoré. *The Tree of Battles of Honoré Bonet* [sic], tr. G.W. Coopland. Liverpool: Liverpool U.P., 1949.

Boulton, D'Arcy Jonathan Dacre. *The Knights of the Crown: The Monarchical Orders of Knighthood in Later Medieval Europe 1325–1520.* Woodbridge: Boydell Press, 2000.

Bradbury, Jim. *The Medieval Siege.* Woodbridge: Boydell Press, 1992.

Contamine, Philippe. "Geoffroy de Charny (début de XIVe siècle–1356), 'Le plus prudhomme et le plus vaillant de tous les autres,'" *Histoire et société: mélanges offerts à Georges Duby.* 2 vols. Aix-en-Provence: Université de Provence, 1992, 2:107–21.

———. *Guerre, état et société à la fin du Moyen Age.* Paris: Mouton, 1972.

Crouch, David. *The Birth of Nobility: Constructing Aristocracy in England and France, 950–1300.* London: Longman, 2005.

———. *Tournament.* London: Hambledon and London, 2005.

Curry, Anne. "The Military Ordinances of Henry V: Texts and Contexts," in Chris Given-Wilson, Ann Kettle and Len Scales (eds.), *War, Government and Aristocracy in the British Isles, c.1150–1500: Essays in Honour of Michael Prestwich.* Woodbridge, UK, Boydell Press: 2008, pp. 214–249.

Duby, Georges. *The Three Orders: Feudal Society Imagined.* Chicago: University of Chicago Press, 1982.

Fallows, Noel. *Jousting in Medieval and Renaissance Iberia.* Woodbridge: Boydell Press, 2010.

Kaeuper, Richard W. *Chivalry and Violence in Medieval Europe.* Oxford: Oxford University Press, 1999.

———. *Holy Warriors: The Religious Ideology of Chivalry.* Philadelphia: University of Pennsylvania Press, 2009 .

Keen, Maurice. *Chivalry.* New Haven: Yale University Press, 1984.

———. *The Laws of War in the Late Middle Ages.* London: Routledge & Kegan Paul, 1965.

Morrillo, Steven. "Expecting Cowardice: Medieval Battle Tactics Reconsidered," *Journal of Medieval Military History* 4 (2006), 65–73.

Muhlberger, Steven. *Deeds of Arms: Formal Combats in the Late Fourteenth Century.* Highland Village TX: Chivalry Bookshelf, 2005.

———. *Jousts and Tournaments: Charny and the Rules for Chivalric Sport in Fourteenth-Century France.* Union City, CA: Chivalry Bookshelf, 2002.

Parker, Geoffrey. "Early Modern Europe," in Michael Howard, George J. Andreopoulos, and Mark R. Shulman. *The Laws of War: Constraints on Warfare in the Western World.* New Haven: Yale University Press, 1994.

———. *Success is Never Final: Empire, War, and Faith in Early Modern Europe.* New York: Basic Books, 2002.

Péristiany, J.G., ed. *Honour and Shame: the Values of Mediterranean Society.* Chicago: University of Chicago Press, 1966.

Ricotti, Ercole. *Storia delle compagnie di ventura in Italia.* 4 vols. Turin: N.P., 1847.

Rodriguez, Jarbel. *Captives and their Saviors in the Medieval Crown of Aragon* Washington, D.C.: Catholic University of America Press, 2007.

Rogers, Clifford J., ed. *The Military Revolution Debate: Readings on the Military Transformation of Early Modern Europe.* Boulder, CO: Westview Press, 1995.

Strickland, Matthew. "Provoking or Avoiding Battle? Challenge, Duel, and Single Combat in Warfare of the High Middle Ages," in *Armies, Chivalry and Warfare in Medieval Britain and France,* ed. Matthew Strickland. Stamford, Lincolnshire: Paul Watkins Publishing, 1998, pp. 335–43.

Sumption, Jonathan., *The Hundred Years War,* vol.2, *Trial by Fire.* Philadelphia: University of Pennsylvania Press, 1999.

Taylor, Andrew. "Chivalric Conversation and the Denial of Male Fear." *Conflicted Identities and Multiple Masculinities: Men in the Medieval West,* ed. Jacqueline Murray. Garland Press: 1999, pp. 169–88.

Van den Neste, Évelyne. *Tournois, joutes, pas d'armes dans les villes de Flandre a la fin du Moyen Âge.* Paris: École des Chartes, 1996.

Wright, Nicholas. *Knights and Peasants: The Hundred Years War in the French Countryside.* Woodbridge: Boydell Press, 1998.

9781937439057